A Patriot for Me

also by John Osborne

Very Like a Whale
West of Suez
The Right Prospectus
Time Present and The Hotel in Amsterdam
A Bond Honoured : A Play
Inadmissible Evidence
Tom Jones : A Film Script
Plays for England : The Blood of the Bambergs and Under Plain Cover
Luther
Look Back in Anger
The Entertainer

Epitaph for George Dillon (with Anthony Creighton)

A Patriot for Me
JOHN OSBORNE

FABER & FABER
3 Queen Square, London

First published in 1966 by
Faber & Faber Limited
3 Queen Square, London WC1
First published in this edition 1971
Printed in Great Britain by
Latimer Trend & Co. Ltd., Whitstable
All rights reserved

All enquiries regarding performing rights should be addressed to Margery Vosper Ltd., 53a Shaftesbury Avenue, London, W.1.

ISBN 0 571 09865 7

This play has not been licensed for public performance by the Lord Chamberlain. A list of the cuts and alterations requested by the Lord Chamberlain – and to which Mr Osborne refused to agree – is printed as an appendix to this volume.

The first performance of A PATRIOT FOR ME was given at the Royal Court Theatre, Sloane Square, London, on 30th June 1965, by the English Stage Society, by arrangement with the English Stage Company. It was directed by Anthony Page and the décor was by Jocelyn Herbert.
The musical adviser was John Addison. The cast was as follows:

ALFRED REDL   Maximilian Schell

AUGUST SICZYNSKI   John Castle

STEINBAUER   Rio Fanning

LUDWIG MAX VON KUPFER   Frederick Jaeger

KUPFER'S SECONDS   Lew Luton, Richard Morgan

PRIVATES   Tim Pearce, David Schurmann, Thick Wilson

LT.-COL. LUDWIG VON MÖHL   Clive Morton

ADJUTANT   Timothy Carlton

MAXIMILIAN VON TAUSSIG   Edward Fox

ALBRECHT   Sandor Eles

WAITERS AT ANNA'S   Peter John, Domy Reiter

OFFICERS   Timothy Carlton, Lew Luton, Hal Hamilton, Richard Morgan

WHORES   Dona Martyn, Virginia Wetherell, Jackie Daryl, Sandra Hampton

ANNA   Laurel Mather

HILDE   Jennifer Jayne

STANITSIN   Desmond Perry

COL. MISCHA OBLENSKY   George Murcell

GEN. CONRAD VON HÖTZENDORF   Sebastian Shaw

COUNTESS SOPHIA DELYANOFF   Jill Bennett

JUDGE ADVOCATE JAROSLAV KUNZ   Ferdy Mayne

FLUNKEYS   John Forbes, Richard Morgan, Peter John, Timothy Carlton

9

HOFBURG GUESTS   Cyril Wheeler, Douglas Sheldon,
                  Bryn Bartlett, Dona Martyn,
                  Virginia Wetherell, Jackie Daryl,
                  Sandra Hampton, Laurel Mather
CAFÉ WAITERS   Anthony Roye, Domy Reiter
                  Bryn Bartlett, Cyril Wheeler
GROUP AT TABLE   Dona Martyn, Laurel Mather,
                  Bryn Bartlett, Cyril Wheeler
YOUNG MAN IN CAFÉ   Paul Robert
PAUL   Douglas Sheldon
PRIVATES   Richard Morgan, David Schurmann, Tim
            Pearce, Thick Wilson
BARON VON EPP   George Devine
FERDY   John Forbes
FIGARO   Thick Wilson
LT. STEFAN KOVACS   Hal Hamilton
MARIE-ANTOINETTE   Lew Luton
TSARINA   Domy Reiter
LADY GODIVA   Peter John
BALL GUESTS   Cyril Wheeler, Richard Morgan,
               Timothy Carlton, John Castle, Edward
               Fox, Paul Robert, Douglas Sheldon,
               Tim Pearce
FLUNKEY   David Schurmann
SHEPHERDESSES   Franco Derosa, Robert Kidd
DR. SCHOEPFER   Vernon Dobtcheff
BOY   Franco Derosa
2ND. LT. VICTOR JERZABEK   Tim Pearce
HOTEL WAITERS   Bryn Bartlett, Lew Luton
ORDERLY   Richard Morgan
MISCHA LIPSCHUTZ   David Schurmann
MITZI HEIGEL   Virginia Wetherell
MINISTER   Anthony Roye
VOICES OF DEPUTIES   Clive Morton, Sebastian Shaw,
                      George Devine, Vernon
                      Dobtcheff, Cyril Wheeler
MUSICAL DIRECTOR   Tibor Kunstler
MUSICIANS   Reg Richman (Bass), Michael Zborowski
             (Piano), Ray Webb (Guitar)

AUSTRIA-HUNGARY
Lemberg, Warsaw, Prague, Dresden, Vienna
1890–1913

ACT I

ACT II

ACT III

ACT I *Scene 1*

A Gymnasium. Of the 7th Galician Infantry Regiment at Lemburg, Galicia, 1890. It appears to be empty. From the high windows on one side, the earliest morning light shows up the climbing bars that run from floor to ceiling. From this, a long, thick rope hangs. Silhouetted is a vaulting horse. The lonely, slow tread of one man's boots is heard presently on the harsh floor. A figure appears. At this stage, his features can barely be made out. It is ALFRED REDL, *at this time Lieutenant. He has close cropped hair, a taut, compact body, a moustache. In most scenes he smokes long black cheroots, like Toscanas. On this occasion, he takes out a shabby cigarette case, an elegant amber holder, inserts a cigarette and lights it thoughtfully. He looks up at the window, takes out his watch and waits. It is obvious he imagines himself alone. He settles down in the half light. A shadow crosses his vision.*

REDL: Who's there? (*Pause.*) Who is it? Come on! Hey!

VOICE: Redl?

REDL: Who is it?

VOICE: Yes. I see you now.

REDL: Siczynski? Is it? Siczynski?

VOICE: Thought it was you. Yes.

> (*A figure appears,* PAUL SICZYNSKI. *He is a strong, very handsome young man about the same age as* REDL, *but much more boyish looking.* REDL *already has the stamp of an older man.*)

SICZYNSKI: Sorry.

REDL: Not at all.

SICZYNSKI: I startled you.

REDL: Well: we're both early.

SICZYNSKI: Yes.

REDL: Still. Not all that much. Cigarette?

(SICZYNSKI *takes one.* REDL *lights it for him.*)

Almost light. I couldn't sleep anyway. Could you?

SICZYNSKI: (*smiles*). I haven't the style for that. Von Kupfer has though. Expect he's snoozing away now. (*Looks at his watch.*) Being wakened by his servant. Um?

REDL: He gave a champagne supper at Anna's.

SICZYNSKI: Who was invited?

REDL: Half the garrison, I imagine.

SICZYNSKI: Did you go?

REDL: I'm your second . . .

SICZYNSKI: Is that what prevented you being asked?

REDL: It would have stopped me going.

SICZYNSKI: Well then, he'll have stayed there till the last moment, I should think. Perhaps he'll have been worn down to nothing by one of those strapping Turkish whores.

REDL: I doubt it.

SICZYNSKI: His spine cracked in between those thighs. Snapped. . . . All the way up. No, you're most likely right. *You're* right.

REDL: He's popular: I suppose.

SICZYNSKI: Yes. Unlikeable too.

REDL: Yes. He's a good, what's he, he's a good officer.

SICZYNSKI: He's a gentleman. And adjutant, adjutant mark you, of a field battery at the ripe old age of twenty-one. He's not half the soldier you are.

REDL: Well . . .

SICZYNSKI: And now he's on his way to the War College.

REDL: (*quick interest.*) Oh?

SICZYNSKI: Of course. If you'd been in his boots, you'd have been in there and out again by this time, you'd be a major at least, by now. (*Pause.*) Sorry—didn't mean to rub it in.

14

REDL: Kupfer. Ludwig Max Von Kupfer . . . it's cold.

SICZYNSKI: Cigarette smoke's warm.

> (*Pause.*)

REDL: How are you?

SICZYNSKI: Cold.

REDL: Here.

SICZYNSKI: Cognac? Your health. Here's to the War College. And you.

REDL: Thank you.

SICZYNSKI: Oh, you will. Get in, I mean. *You* just have to pack in all the effort, while the Kupfers make none at all. He'll be sobering up by now. Putting his aristocratic head under the cold tap and shouting in that authentic Viennese drawl at whoever's picking up after him. You'd better, make it, I mean. Or you'll spend the rest of it in some defeated frontier town with debts. And more debts to look forward to as you go on. Probably the gout. (*Pause.*) I just hope there isn't ever a war.

> (*They smoke in silence. Slightly shy, tense.*
> SICZYNSKI *leans against the vaulting horse.*)

REDL: You may underestimate Kupfer.

SICZYNSKI: Maybe. But then he overestimates himself. *You*'ve tremendous resources, reserves, energy. You won't let any old waters close over your head without a struggle first.

REDL: What about you?

SICZYNSKI: (*smiles*). I'm easily disheartened.

REDL: He's destructive, *very* destructive.

SICZYNSKI: Who?

REDL: Kupfer.

SICZYNSKI: Yes, yes. And wilful. Coldly, not too cold, not disinterested.

REDL: That's why I think you underestimate him.

SICZYNSKI: But more vicious than most. You're right there. He's a killer all right.

REDL: Someone'll chalk him up . . . sometime.

SICZYNSKI: What about me?

REDL: That would be very good. Very good.

SICZYNSKI: Just not very likely . . .

REDL: Have you done this before?

SICZYNSKI: (*smiles*). No, never. Have you?

REDL: Only as a bystander.

SICZYNSKI: Well, this time you're a participant. . . . I'd always expected to *be* challenged a hundred times. I never thought *I'd* do it. Well, picked the right man. Only the wrong swordsman. May I?
(*He indicated Cognac.* REDL *nods.*)
Have you seen him?

REDL: Seen? Oh, with a sabre. No. Have you?

SICZYNSKI: No. Have you seen *me*?

REDL: Often.

SICZYNSKI: Well, there it is.

REDL: (*softly*). More times than I can think of.

SICZYNSKI: They say only truly illiterate minds are obdurate. Well, that's me and Kupfer.

REDL: Why do you feel like this about him? He's not exactly untypical.

SICZYNSKI: Not by any means. For me, well, perhaps he just plays the part better. He makes me want to be sick. Over *him* preferably.

REDL: I don't understand you. You're more than a match for his sort.

SICZYNSKI: I just chose the wrong ground to prove it, here.
(*Pause.*)

REDL: Look, Siczynski, why don't I, I'm quite plausible and not half a bad actor, for one . . . reason and another, why don't you let me, sort of . . .

SICZYNSKI: Thank you, Redl. You can't do anything now.

REDL: Very well.

SICZYNSKI: Don't be offended.

REDL: Why should I?

SICZYNSKI: (wry). Someone who looks as good as me
ought to be able to handle himself a bit better,
don't you agree?

REDL: Yes.

SICZYNSKI: At least—physically. . . . A *little* better don't
you think? Why did you agree to be my second?

REDL: Why did you ask me?

SICZYNSKI: I thought you'd agree to. Did you get
anyone else?

REDL: Steinbauer.

SICZYNSKI: As a favour to you? No, I didn't think you'd
have to be persuaded.

REDL: No.

SICZYNSKI: Mine's gone out.
(REDL *offers him a cigarette, from which he takes a
light.*)
I thought you always smoked those long Italian
cigars.
(REDL *nods.*)
Expensive taste. What is it?

REDL: I was only going to ask you: *are* you a Jew?

SICZYNSKI: (smiles). Grandmother. Maternal Grandmother. Quite enough though, don't you think? Oh,
she became Catholic when she married my Grandfather. Not that she ever took it seriously, any more
than him. She'd a good sense of fun, not like the
rest of my family. You think it doesn't matter about
Kupfer's insult, don't you? Well of course you're
right. I don't think it would have mattered *what* he
said. Oh, I quite enjoyed his jokes about calling me
Rothschild. What *I* objected to, from him,—in the
circumstances, was being called Fräulein Rothschild
. . . .

REDL: You shouldn't gamble.

SICZYNSKI: I don't.

REDL: On people's goodwill.

SICZYNSKI: I don't. *You* do.

REDL: I do? No, I don't . . . I try not to.
  (*He is confused for a moment.* SICZYNSKI *watches him thoughtfully, through his cigarette smoke. It is getting lighter, colder.*)
SICZYNSKI: You smell of peppermints.
REDL: Nearly time. (*He stands.*)
SICZYNSKI: Kupfer's breath stinks.
REDL: I hadn't noticed.
SICZYNSKI: You mean you haven't got near enough? You don't need to. *He* should chew peppermints.
  (*Pause.*)
  Have some of your brandy.
REDL: Thanks.
SICZYNSKI: It's a cold time to be up, to be up at all.
REDL: I've hardly ever had warm feet. Not since I went to Cadet School.
SICZYNSKI: You work too hard.
REDL: What else can I do?
SICZYNSKI: Sorry. Of course, you're right. I'm just waiting. Can't think much any more.
  (REDL *would like to help if there were some means. But he can't.*)
  Go on. If you can, I mean. Don't if you can't . . . Won't be long, now . . .
REDL: We've never talked together much, have we? We must have both been here? What? Two years?
SICZYNSKI: Why couldn't you sleep?
REDL: Don't know. Oh yes, I had a dream . . .
SICZYNSKI: But then you're not what they call sociable, are you?
REDL: Aren't I?
SICZYNSKI: Well! Asking for extra duties, poring over all those manuals.
REDL: You don't make it sound very likeable.
SICZYNSKI: It isn't—much.
  (REDL *takes out his watch.*)

REDL: I told Steinbauer two minutes before. He's pretty reliable.

SICZYNSKI: Anyway, you're taking a risk doing *this*. But I suppose Kupfer will draw the fire.

REDL: And you. You specially.

SICZYNSKI: The Galician Jew, you mean? Yes. But that's only if I win.

REDL: It needn't come to that.

SICZYNSKI: It will.

REDL: I'll see it doesn't.

SICZYNSKI: No, you won't. You can't. . . . What, what does one, do you suppose, well, look for in anyone, anyone else, I mean.

REDL: For?

SICZYNSKI: Elsewhere.

REDL: I haven't tried. Or thought about it. At least . . .

SICZYNSKI: I mean: That isn't clearly, really, clearly, already in oneself?

REDL: Nothing, I expect.

    (*Pause.*)

SICZYNSKI: Tell me about your dream.

REDL: Do you believe in dreams?

SICZYNSKI: Not specially. They're true while they last, I suppose.

REDL: Well, it wasn't—

    (*There is the sound of boots. Walking swiftly, confidently, this time. The two men look at each other.*)

    Steinbauer. On the dot.

    (STEINBAUER *enters.*)

    Morning, Steinbauer.

    (STEINBAUER *nods, slightly embarrassed. Clicks his heels at* SICZYNSKI.

    Cold.

STEINBAUER: Yes.

SICZYNSKI: Got the cutlery? Oh, yes I see.

STEINBAUER: All here.

SICZYNSKI: Redl was telling me his dream. Go on.

REDL: It's nothing.

SICZYNSKI: That hardly matters, does it?

REDL: Not really time.

SICZYNSKI: Please.

(STEINBAUER *takes out his watch.*)

REDL: Just, oh, I was, well later, I was, I won't tell you
the first—

SICZYNSKI: Why not?

REDL: It's too dull. So is *this* too. Anyway: I was
attending a court martial. Not mine. Someone
else's. I don't quite know whose. But a friend of
some sort, someone I liked. Someone upright, frank,
respected, but upright. It was quite clear from the
start what the outcome would be, and I was
immediately worrying about having to go and visit
him in gaol. And it wasn't just because I knew I
would be arrested myself as soon as I got in there.
It wasn't for that. Anyhow, there I was, and I
went and started to talk to him. He didn't say
anything. There was just the wire netting between
us . . . and then of course, they arrested *me*. I
couldn't tell whether he was pleased or not.
Pleased that I'd come to see him or that they'd got
me too. They touched me on the shoulder and told
me to stand up, which I did. And by that time he'd
gone. Somehow.

*(Sound of several pairs of boots clattering on the
unyielding floor into the Gymnasium.* REDL *frowns
anxiously at* SICZYNSKI, *who smiles at him. As soon as*
KUPFER *and his seconds arrive, they get to their feet.
Both sides salute each other and prepare for the duel in
silence. Sabres are selected. Tunics discarded, etc. All
brisk. The duel begins. The four men watch almost
indifferently at first. But the spectacle soon strips away this.
Blood is drawn, sweat runs, breathing tightens. At one
point* REDL *steps forward.* KUPFER *orders him back
curtly. All settle down for the end. It comes fairly soon.*

SICZYNSKI *cries out and falls to the ground.* KUPFER
*begins dressing almost immediately. He goes out with his
companions, who are trying to be composed.*)
STEINBAUER: Shall I? Yes, I'd better get the doctor.
REDL: Yes, I suppose so.
(STEINBAUER *follows the others out.* REDL *wipes the
blood from* SICZYNSKI's *mouth, cradling him in his arms.
He is clearly dead.*)

FADE

Scene 2

*Office of the Commandant, Seventh Galician Infantry Regiment.
The Commandant, LIEUTENANT-COLONEL VON MÖHL, is
seated at his desk. A sharp rap at the door. VON MÖHL grunts.
The door is opened smartly by the ADJUTANT.*

ADJUTANT: Lieutenant Redl, sir.
(REDL *enters, salutes, etc.*)
MÖHL: Is Taussig there?
ADJUTANT: Yes, sir.
MÖHL: Good. All right.
(ADJUTANT *goes out.*)
Redl, Redl, Redl: yes. (*He looks up.*) Sit down, please.
(REDL *sits.* MÖHL *scrutinises him.*)
Well, Redl. You've quite a good deal of news to
come it seems to me. Yes.
REDL: Yes, sir?
MÖHL: You may think that a young officer gets lost
among all the others, that he isn't observed,
constantly, critically and sympathetically. You
might think that an officer with an unremarkable
background, or without rather dazzling connections
of one sort or another would go unnoticed. Do you
think that, Redl?
REDL: Sir, my own experience is that genuine merit
rarely goes unnoticed or unrewarded. Even,
particularly in the Army.
MÖHL: Good. And quite correct, Redl, and for a very
obvious reason. The future of the Empire depends
on the Army, probably the future of Europe, on an

22

alert, swift machine that can meet instant crisis
from whatever quarter it may come. It's taken us a
long time to learn our lesson, lessons like Solferino.
Expensive, humiliating and inglorious, but worth it
now. Only the very best kind of men can be
entrusted in the modern army.

(*He waves at the map of pre-1914 Europe, with Austria-
Hungary in the middle, behind him.*)

No one's going to be passed over, every man'll have
his chance to prove himself, show what he could do,
given half the chance. I don't say there still aren't
short cuts for people who don't apparently deserve
it, but that's not for you or me to argue. What we
can do is make sure the way's made to virgin merit,
someone with nothing else. What do you say?

REDL: I'm sure you're right, sir.

MÖHL: Oh?

REDL: It always seems quite clear to me, sir, the
officers who complain about privilege are invariably
inferior or mediocre.

(REDL *speaks coolly and carefully. He is anxious to be
courteous and respectful without seeming unctuous, or
sound a false, fawning note. He succeeds.*)

MÖHL: Exactly. The real good 'uns don't ever really get
left out, that's why so much nonsense is talked,
especially about the Army. You can't *afford* to
ignore a good man. He's too valuable. A good
soldier always knows another one. That's what
comradeship is. It's not an empty thing, not an
empty thing at all. It's knowing the *value* of other
men. And cherishing it. Now: Redl. Two reasons I
sent for you. I'll, yes, we'll, I think we'll deal with
the best first.

(*He pauses.* REDL *waits.*)

As you know, as Commander, it's my duty to
recommend officers for War College examination.
This year I only felt able to recommend Von

Taussig, Von Kupfer, and yourself. The result I can now tell you, after the final examination and interview, is that you have all three been granted admission, a very fine achievement for us all. Four hundred and eighteen candidates for thirty-nine places. Well, Von Taussig has been admitted number twenty-eight, yourself twenty-six and Von Kupfer seventeen. Congratulations.

REDL: Thank you, sir.

MÖHL: Well, I'm very pleased indeed myself, with the result. All three accepted. It's quite something for me too, you know, especially over you. I was pretty sure about the other two, well, of course. . . . But you, well, I knew you had the education, enough . . . There it is. Now you've done it.

REDL: I'm very grateful, sir.

MÖHL: By yourself. You. Number twenty-six! Please. Smoke, if you wish. Here—one of these.
(*Offers him a cigar. Takes one himself.* REDL *lights both of them.*)
So: How do you feel?

REDL: Very proud—and grateful, sir.

MÖHL: I don't think you realise, you've made quite an impression. Here, listen to this. Arithmetic, algebra, geometry, trigonometry—all excellent. Elementary engineering, construction, fortification, geography and international law, all eighty-five per cent, all first class. Riding—required standard. That's the only begrudging remark on any of your reports, required standard. Anyway, get that horse out in the school a bit. Yes?

REDL: Yes, sir.

MÖHL: Let's see now, what does it say, do you speak Russian?

REDL: No, sir.

MÖHL: No matter. You will. Native language?

REDL: Ruthenian.

MÖHL: German—excellent. Polish, French—fair.
Punctilious knowledge military and international
matters. Seems to know Franco-Prussian campaign
better than anyone who actually took part. Learned.
All the qualities of first-class field officer and an
unmistakable flair for intelligence. No. Wait a
minute, there's more yet. Upright, discreet, frank
and open, painstaking, marked ability to anticipate,
as well as initiate instructions, without being
reckless, keen judgement, cool under pressure—
that's Erdmannsdorfer, so that's good, very good
indeed—Yes, cool, fine interpreter of the finest
modern military thinking. Personality: friendly but
unassertive, dignified and strikes everyone as the
type of a gentleman and distinguished officer of
the Royal and Imperial Army. Well, what do you
say?

REDL: I'm overwhelmed, sir.

MÖHL: Well, I like to see this sort of thing happen.
Kupfer and Taussig are one thing, and I'm proud
of them. But you're another. . . . Yours is effort,
effort, concerted, sustained, intelligent effort.
Which: brings me to the Siczynski affair. Of course,
you realise that if your part in that incident had
been made properly known, it would almost
certainly have prejudiced your application?

REDL: Yes, sir.

MÖHL: However, we chose to be discreet.

REDL: I'm more grateful than I can tell you, sir.

MÖHL: Well, of course, with Kupfer, it was more
difficult. However, he has been in trouble of this
kind before, and, let's be honest about it, he does
have advantages. He is able to get away with
incidents like Siczynski occasionally, though even he
can't do it too often. Of course, he was a principal
in this case and you weren't, but I must tell you it
was a grave error on your part ever to have

consented to become involved in an affair which
ends in a brother officer's death. I'm saying this to
you as a warning for the future. *Don't* get
involved.

REDL: Yes, sir. May I ask where is Lieutenant Von
Kupfer, sir?

MÖHL: Temporarily transferred to Wiener Neustadt. . . .
Was Siczynski a friend of yours?

REDL: No, sir.

MÖHL: What was your opinion of him?

REDL: I hardly knew him, sir. (*Realises quickly he needs
to provide more than this.*) He struck me as being
hyper-critical, over-sceptical about things.

MÖHL: What things?

REDL: Army life and traditions, esprit——

MÖHL: Religion?

REDL: We never discussed it. But—yes, I suspect so, I
should think . . .

MÖHL: Jewish . . .?

REDL: Yes, sir. I believe.

MÖHL: Galician, like yourself.

REDL: Yes.

MÖHL: You're yes, Catholic, of course.

REDL: Yes, sir.

MÖHL: What about women?

REDL: Siczynski?

(*Nod from* MÖHL.)

As I say, I didn't know him well.

MÖHL: But?

REDL: I never thought of him, no one seemed to, as a
ladies' man.

MÖHL: Precisely. Yet he was very attractive, physically,
wouldn't you say?

REDL: That's a hard question for another man to
answer——

MÖHL: Oh, come, Redl, you know what women are
attracted——

26

REDL: Yes. Of course, I should say he was, quite
certainly.

MÖHL: But you never heard of any particular girl or
girls?

REDL: No. But then, we weren't exactly, and I don't——

MÖHL: You are a popular officer—Redl—Siczynski
wasn't. He had debts, too. And quite hefty ones.
Oh, one expects all young officers to have debts.
It's always been so, and always will, till they pay
soldiers properly. Every other week, a fund has
to be raised for this one or that. Fine. But this
officer had, or so it seems, and frankly it doesn't
surprise me, no friends, was in the hands of
moneylenders, of his own race, naturally, and why?
Women? Of course, one asks. But who? No one
knows. No family. Who was worth nine thousand
kroner in debts.

REDL: Nine . . .

MÖHL: Do you think I can find out? It *is* odd, after all.
Young officer, apparently attractive in many ways,
work excellent, intelligence exceptional, diligent,
manly disposition and all the rest of it. Then:
where are you?

REDL: Perhaps?—I don't think he was ever in his right
element.

MÖHL: Well. There it is. Incident closed now, including
your part in it.

REDL: Thank you, sir.

MÖHL: Only remember. Involvement. Debts—well,
you'll be all right. Also, you have friends, and *will*
have. As for women, I think you know what you're
doing.

REDL: I hope so, sir.

MÖHL: What about marriage?

REDL: I'm not contemplating it, not for quite some
time, that is.

MÖHL: Good. You've got ideals and courage and

fortitude, and I'm proud and delighted you'll be going from this regiment to War College. You're on your way, Redl. Taussig!

(ADJUTANT *enters*.)

Send in Taussig.

(ADJUTANT *clicks heels. Enter* TAUSSIG *presently*.)

Ah, Taussig. Come in. You know Redl. You two should have something to celebrate together tonight.

FADE

Scene 3

ANNA's. *A private cubicle. In the background a gipsy orchestra, and flash young officers eating, drinking, swearing, singing, entertaining* ANNA's *young ladies.* REDL *is alone in the cubicle. He leans forward, scoops a champagne bottle from its bucket to pour himself another glass. It is empty. He draws the curtain aside and bawls into the smoke and noise.*

REDL: Anna! Anna! Hey! You! What's your name?!
Max! Leo! Anna! Damn!
(He gives up. Looks in his tunic for his cigar case. Takes one out, a long black Italian cheroot. A YOUNG WAITER *enters.)*
Ah, there you are. Thank God. Another—please.
Oh—you've got it. That's clever.
WAITER: I guessed you'd be wanting another, sir.
REDL: Good fellow. Open it, would you?
WAITER: At once, sir.
REDL: Which one are you then?
WAITER: Which one, sir?
REDL: You're not Leo or that other stumpy creature, what's his name—
WAITER: I am Albrecht, sir.
REDL: You're new then.
WAITER: Seven months, sir.
REDL: Oh. I didn't notice you.
WAITER: You don't often do us the honour, sir.
REDL: Light this for me.
(WAITER does so.)
I can't afford time for this sort of caper very often.

WAITER: What a magnificent cigar case, sir.

REDL: What? Oh. Yes. Present. From my uncle.

WAITER: Very fine indeed. Shall I pour it now?

REDL: Yes.

WAITER: Pol Roger eighty one, sir.

REDL: (*shortly*). Fine.

WAITER: Would that be crocodile, sir?

REDL: Eh? Oh. Yes. Have you see my guest anywhere
among that mob?

WAITER: Lieutenant Taussig, sir?

REDL: Well, who else?

WAITER: He is talking with Madame Anna.
(REDL *sips his champagne. The* WAITER *has increased
his restless, uneasy mood. He can't bring himself to
dismiss him yet.*)

REDL: Rowdy, roaring mob you've got in there.

WAITER: Yes, sir.

REDL: Why do they have to make such a damned show?
Howling and vomiting or whoring.
(*They listen.*)
Drunk. . . . Why do they need to get so drunk?

WAITER: End of the summer manoeuvres they tell me,
sir. Always the same then.

REDL: This place'll get put out of bounds one day.
Someone should warn Anna.

WAITER: I think she just does her best to please the
young officers, sir. Giving them what they ask for.

REDL: They'll get it too, and no mistake. What's that
young officer's name?

WAITER: Which one, sir? Oh, with the red-haired girl,
Hilde—yes, Lieutenant Steinbauer, sir.

REDL: So it is.

WAITER: Very beautiful girl, sir.

REDL: Yes.

WAITER: Very popular, that one.

REDL: Garbage often is.

WAITER: That's true too, of course, sir.

(*Pause.*)

REDL: Taussig! Where the hell is he?

WAITER: Shall I tell him you want him, sir?

REDL: No. Better not. I'm getting bored sitting here on my own.

WAITER: Can I do anything else, sir?

REDL: No. (*Detaining him.*) Do you remember Kupfer?

WAITER: Lieutenant Kupfer? Oh yes, he used to be in here nearly every night, sometimes when he shouldn't have been. We were sorry when he was re-posted.

REDL: And Lieutenant Siczynski? Do you remember him?

WAITER: No, sir, I don't.

REDL: You don't come from Lemberg?

WAITER: No, sir. From Vienna. Oh, you mean the one who was killed in the duel? He used to come in sometimes, usually on his own. But no one seemed to take much notice of him. He didn't exactly avail himself of the place. Like Lieutenant Kupfer. *He* used to have this cubicle regularly.

REDL: You must miss Vienna.

WAITER: I do, sir. There are always so many different things to do *there*. In Lemberg everybody knows who you are and everything about you. . . . Well, no doubt you'll be in Vienna yourself before long. May I congratulate you, sir?

REDL: Thank you.

WAITER: On the General Staff, I've no doubt, sir.

REDL: We'll see.

(*A roar and banging of tables.*)

What the devil's going on?

WAITER: Lieutenant Steinbauer has passed out, sir. They're passing him over their heads . . . One by one . . . Now he's being sick. I'd better go.

REDL: Well, he's better off: see someone takes him home, if you can.

31

WAITER: I'll do my best, sir. So, as I say, you'll soon be seeing for yourself.

REDL: What?

WAITER: Why, Vienna.

REDL: Oh. All I'll see is work. Maps, tactical field work, riding drill, Russian language, maps.

WAITER: Oh, of course.

REDL: That'll be enough for me.

WAITER: Yes, sir.

(*Pause. Enter* TAUSSIG.)

TAUSSIG: Well, I've fixed us up.

REDL: What?

TAUSSIG: Girls. One each. I've been arguing ten minutes with Anna, and she insisted she'd only got one spare, that lovely great black gipsy with the mole on her cheek. There.

WAITER: Zoe.

TAUSSIG: That's the one. So I said to her, I know she's a big girl, but I know my friend Lieutenant Redl won't go much on sharing, especially on an occasion like this evening.

REDL: Please forget it. I'm bored with the place.

TAUSSIG: So am I. We'll take another, oh, you've got another, we'll take some more champagne upstairs with us and be entertained properly, me by big black Zoe, and you, you my friend by Hilde. And very lucky you are, doubly lucky, because she was tied up by young Steinbauer until a few moments ago, but he's now safely on his face in the cellar, he won't be capable of fulfilling his little engagement tonight, he'll be lucky to stand up on parade in the morning, and Hilde, red, pale, vacant and booked this moment by me is all yours.

REDL: It doesn't matter.

TAUSSIG: Of course, it doesn't. It's all fixed. Fixed by me and paid for.

REDL: Taussig, I can't allow it.

TAUSSIG: Nonsense. It's done.

(WAITER *pours champagne.* TAUSSIG *drinks.*)

You insisted on buying the dinner and champagne. And now, *more* champagne. Now, *I* insist on treating you. Your health.

(*He glances quickly at the* WAITER.)

To black Zoe and her gipsy mole. And Hilde and her red whatever special she's got in there. Drink up.

(REDL *drinks.*)

(*to* WAITER): What are *you* standing about for?

REDL: He was opening the champagne.

TAUSSIG: Well, take another one up. On *my* bill.

REDL: Are you sure?

TAUSSIG: Of course I'm sure. We're going to need it. Come on, I'm glad to see you smoking a cigar again. Can't stand the smell of those peppermints. I've always wanted to tell you. I say, that's a pretty classy case.

REDL: My uncle.

TAUSSIG: I didn't know you had rich relatives.

REDL: Only him.

TAUSSIG: Perhaps I should have let you pay for Hilde yourself.

REDL: Of course. Please.

TAUSSIG: Unless you *would* have preferred Zoe. Sharing, I mean.

REDL: Hilde sounds just the thing.

TAUSSIG: I think she's more your type. Bit on the skinny side. No bottom, little tiny bottom, not a real roly-poly. And breasts made like our friend here. Go on, go and get that other bottle!

REDL: (*to* WAITER). Just a moment.

TAUSSIG: I'll round them up.

(*Pause.*)

Don't be all night then.

REDL: Just coming.

(*He goes to his wallet, trying not to be awkward. He
hands a note to the* WAITER.)

WAITER: Thank you, sir.

(*He lights a match for* REDL, *who looks up. Then
notices his cigar is out.*)

REDL: Oh, yes.

WAITER: Shall I take this bottle up then, sir?

REDL: Yes. Wait a minute.

(WAITER *pauses.*)

Pour me another glass.

(*He does so. Picks up bucket.*)

WAITER: Good night, sir.

REDL: Good night.

(*The* WAITER *goes out.* REDL *stares into his glass,
then drains it, fastens his tunic smartly and steps through
the curtain into the tumult.*

FADE

34

Scene 4

ANNA's. *An upstairs room. Bare save for a bed. Lying on it are* HILDE *and* REDL. *Only the outline of their bodies is visible. In the darkness* REDL's *cigar glows. Silence. Then there is an occasional noise from one of the other rooms.*

HILDE: (*whispers*). Hullo. (*Pause.*) Hullo.

REDL: Yes.

HILDE: Alfred! Can't you sleep?

REDL: No. I'm not tired.

HILDE: You slept a little. Oh, not for long. Can I get you anything?

REDL: No thank you.

HILDE: You clench your teeth. Did you know that?

REDL: No.

HILDE: When you're asleep. It makes quite a noise. Scraping together.

REDL: I'm sorry.

HILDE: Oh, please. I didn't mean that. But it'll wear your teeth down. And you've got such nice teeth. You smell of peppermints. Can I put the light on?

REDL: It's your room.

HILDE: It's yours tonight.
  (*She lights the lamp.*)
  Some men's mouths are disgusting.

REDL: I'm sure.

HILDE: You look better. You almost fainted. Can't I get you anything? (*Pause.*) Is there any champagne left?
  (*He pours her some from beside the bed.*)
  Don't often get champagne bought me. Well, here's to Vienna. Wish I was going.

35

REDL: Why don't you?

HILDE: I shall, I'm saving up.

REDL: What will you do—the same thing—when you get there?

HILDE: I suppose so. Do you know, your eyes are like mine?

REDL: Are they?

HILDE: I've never seen a man faint before.

REDL: You should be in the army. Do you want to get married?

HILDE: (*softly*). Yes. Of course. Why? Are you proposing?

REDL: I've seen what you've got to offer.

HILDE: Only just. I'm sorry.

REDL: What about?

HILDE: You don't like me.

REDL: What *are* you on about?

HILDE: Never mind. More warm champagne, please.
(*He pours.*)

REDL: What do you mean? Eh?

HILDE: Nothing. Thank you. God bless. And I hope you'll, you'll be happy in Vienna.

REDL: I'm sorry. Those exams and things have taken it out of me. Perhaps I'll come back tomorrow.

HILDE: Was Lieutenant Siczynski a friend of yours?

REDL: No. Why, did you know him?

HILDE: I used to see him.

REDL: Did he——

HILDE: No. Not with anyone. He usually sat on his own in a corner, reading the foreign papers or just drinking. I used to look at his eyes. But he never looked at me.
(REDL *leans over the bed and kisses her lingeringly. She returns the embrace abstractedly. He looks down at her.*)
Peppermints!

REDL: Damn it! I apologised, didn't I?
(*She puts her finger to his mouth to calm him.*)

HILDE: *And* cigars. That's what you smell of, and horses and saddles. What could be nicer, and more manly?

REDL: You're very, very pretty, Hilde. I love your red hair.

HILDE: You don't have to make love to me, Alfred. I'm only a whore.

REDL: But I mean it.

HILDE: Hired by your friend.

REDL: Pretty little, brittle bones.

HILDE: Lieutenant Taussig.

REDL: Is that him, next door?

HILDE: (*listens*). At this moment, I should say.
(*They listen.*)
Is he a good friend of yours?

REDL: I can't say I'd call anyone I know a good friend.

HILDE: Are you sure you can't sleep?

REDL: Yes . . . But why don't you?

HILDE: May I put my head on your arm?

REDL: If you wish . . .

HILDE: No, I'll finish my champagne. Do you like children?

REDL: Yes. Why?

HILDE: Would you like some of your own?

REDL: Very much. Wouldn't you?

HILDE: Yes, I would.

REDL: Then what's stopping you?

HILDE: One would like to be loved, if it's possible.

REDL: Love's hardly ever possible.

HILDE: Do you believe that?

REDL: Yes. Anyway, there are always too many babies being born. So—

HILDE: You may be right. Perhaps that's why you're in the army.

REDL: What's the matter with you? I'm in the army because it suits *me* and I'm suited to *it*. I can make my own future. I can style it my own way.

37

HILDE: What about Siczynski?

REDL: He wasn't suited to it. Who's in that other room, there?

HILDE: Albrecht . . . Would you like to go?

REDL: No. I just asked you a question, that's all. Albrecht who?

HILDE: The waiter you were talking to while I was with the young lieutenant.

(*Pause.*)

REDL: He's a noisy fellow.

HILDE: Or whoever's with him.

(*They listen. She watches* REDL's *face.*)

Your cigar's gone out. Here. He always gets the pick, Albrecht. Anything he wants. Anyone.

(*She moves over to the wall and pulls back a flap and looks through.*)

Come here.

REDL: What for?

(*But he joins her.*)

HILDE: Do you want to look?

(*He hesitates, then does so. She returns to the bed, empties the champagne into her glass, and watches him. Presently, he turns away and sits on the bed. She puts her arm round his shoulder. Offers him drink.*)

Have some?

(*He shakes his head.*)

Sad?

REDL: No. Not sad. One always just wishes that a congenial evening had been—even more congenial.

HILDE: Think I'll go to bed. It's made me sleepy again.

(REDL *listens.*)

Shall I turn the light out?

(*He nods. She does so. He goes to the window and looks out. Presently—*

Good night, Alfred.

REDL: Good night, Hilde.

HILDE: Sorry. I can't keep awake. But you don't
   mind . . .
   (*He looks across at her, puts on his tunic, takes out a bank
   note, picks up his cap.*)
REDL: Good night, Hilde. Thank you.
   (*He presses the note into her hand.*)
HILDE: I'll tell your friend you left in time for reveille.
   (*He turns.*)
   Alfred——
   (*She sits up and kisses him lightly.*)
   You have the most beautiful mouth that ever, ever
   kissed me. Good night, Lieutenant.
REDL: Good night.
HILDE: (*sleepily*). You'll be a colonel one day. On the
   General Staff. Or even a general.
   (*He gazes down at her, re-lights his cigar. The noise from
   the adjoining room has subsided. He slips out.*) .

FADE

Scene 5

Warsaw. A darkened office. The light from a magic lantern shines white on a blank screen which faces the audience. A figure is seen to be operating it. Another, seated in front of it, is watching the screen. The first figure is LIEUTENANT STANITSIN. *The second* COLONEL OBLENSKY.

OBLENSKY: Next!

STANITSIN: Redl.

> (REDL's *photograph in uniform on the screen.*)
> Alfred Von Redl. Captain. Seventh Galician Infantry Regiment. Lemberg. Born Lemberg March 4th, 1864. Family background: parents Leopold and Marthe Redl. Eighth of eleven children. Father ex-horse trooper, now second-grade clerical worker Royal and Imperial Railway. Religion: Catholic. Education: Cadet School, passed out with honours. Equitation school.

OBLENSKY: Oh, do get to the meat, Stanitsin. I want my dinner.

STANITSIN: (*flustered slightly*). Oh—just——

OBLENSKY: If there is any. They're not a very promising lot this time, are they?

STANITSIN: Passed out of War College May of last year, number twenty-three of his entry, recommended particularly, on pink paper, recommended.

OBLENSKY: (*turns head*). So it is. Meticulous.

STANITSIN: For appointment on General Staff.

OBLENSKY: Yes.

STANITSIN: Health: periodic asthma while at Cadet

School, twice almost leading to his discharge. However, in the past ten years, this complaint seems to have been almost completely overcome. Contracted syphilis two and a half years ago, underwent treatment and discharged Lemberg Military Hospital. One serious breach of discipline, involved in duel when fellow officer was killed. Acted as one of the officer's seconds. Affair hushed up and Redl reprimanded. Otherwise unblemished record sheet. Present duty: shortly returned from nine months on staff of Military Attaché in St. Petersburg, ostensibly learning Russian language.

OBLENSKY: Probably all he did do. That's all *ours* do in Vienna. Pick up German in that atrocious, affected accent. I don't know why either of us bothers to observe—just young officers going to diplomatic functions, learning the language painstakingly, like an English governess, and about as well, and not a secret in sight. Most of them just come back like Redl, with the clap at least, or someone else's crabs. Well?

STANITSIN: Waiting for new posting. Financial affairs: No source of income apart from army pay. Although he seems to have invented a fond uncle who occasionally gives him fancy presents or gratuities, of whom there is no trace. Debts, not exactly serious, are considerable. They include: tailor, the biggest trade debt, outstanding accounts at various cafés, restaurants, bootmakers, livery, wine merchants and cigar—

OBLENSKY: Oh, come along, friend. What else?

STANITSIN: Not much. Two moneylenders, small, Fink, Miklas also.

OBLENSKY: Oh—Miklas. I know him. How much?

STANITSIN: Together, some twenty-two hundred kronen.

OBLENSKY: Yes?

STANITSIN: He is also negotiating the lease of a third-floor apartment in the Eighth District.

OBLENSKY: Yes?

STANITSIN: That's about it.

OBLENSKY: Personal?

STANITSIN: Studious. Popular with fellow officers.

OBLENSKY: Oh, come along: women?

STANITSIN: Occasionally. Nothing sustained.

OBLENSKY: Spare time?

STANITSIN: Work mostly. Otherwise cafés, reading foreign newspapers, drinking with friends.

OBLENSKY: All army?

STANITSIN: Mostly.

OBLENSKY: Languages?

STANITSIN: Ruthenian native. Polish, German, some French.

OBLENSKY: And Russian. Some. Yes?

STANITSIN: I'm sorry?

OBLENSKY: What else? If anything.

STANITSIN: That's all, sir.

OBLENSKY: All right. Clever, brilliant officer, unpromising background. Ambitious. Bit extravagant. Popular. Diligent. What do you want to do?

STANITSIN: Continue surveillance, sir?

OBLENSKY: Unpromising lot. Very well. Get me a drink. Ah—good. Redl. Yes. All right. Background: nil. Prospects of brilliant military career exceptional. What he needs now, at this exact stage, is a good, advantageous marriage. An heiress is the ideal. But a rich widow would do even better. He probably needs someone specially adroit socially, a good listener, sympathetic, a woman other men are pleased to call a friend and mean it. Experienced. He knows what he wants, I dare say. He just needs someone to unobtrusively provide the right elements. . . . Perhaps we should think about it. . . .

42

Anyway, remind me—sometime next week. Right.
Come on then. Next!

STANITSIN: Kupfer.

(REDL's *photograph is switched abruptly from the screen
and replaced by* KUPFER's.)

Kupfer. Ludwig Max Von Kupfer. Major.

FADE

Scene 6

A terrace in the Hofburg, the Emperor's residence in Vienna. Through the french windows, naturally, is where the court ball is going on, with the aristocracy, diplomatic corps, officers of the Royal and Imperial Army, Flunkeys, etc. Talking to VON MÖHL *is Chief of the General staff, General* CONRAD VON HÖTZENDORF.

MÖHL: Haven't been here for years.

HÖTZENDORF: Oh?

MÖHL: It's good to be back.

HÖTZENDORF: I'm sure.

MÖHL: There's nowhere quite like it, really, is there?

HÖTZENDORF: No. There's not.

MÖHL: Not where I've been, anyway. What about you, General?

HÖTZENDORF: No, no I don't think so.

MÖHL: I haven't been here since, oh, well, when was it, well I was a young captain, and I was in the Railway Bureau.

HÖTZENDORF: Were you?

MÖHL: Wiry. I could bend, do anything. Like a willow. Where's your wife, General? Would you like me—

HÖTZENDORF: No. She's all right. She's somewhere . . . Paris, that's the nearest to it, I suppose.

MÖHL: Yes.

HÖTZENDORF: But really, altogether different.

MÖHL: Entirely.

HÖTZENDORF: In Vienna, well, everyone is bourgeois, or

44

whatever it is, and a good thing too, everyone, the beggars in the street, kitchen maids, the aristocracy and, let's be honest, the Emperor.

MÖHL: Yes.

HÖTZENDORF: And they all of them enjoy themselves. In Paris, well, in my experience, they're all pretending to be bohemians, from top to bottom, and all the time, every one of them are tradesmen. Well, I don't think you're a real bohemian if you've one eye—or *both* eyes in the case of Paris—on the cash box.

MÖHL: Quite.

HÖTZENDORF: Yes. That's Paris. That's the French. Trouble with Vienna: seems to have old age built into it.

MÖHL: Still, that's better than moving on to God knows what, *and* in such an ugly way, like Prussia, for instance.

HÖTZENDORF: Yes. Or England. Even more. They'll soon wreck it. Prussians *are* efficient. English wilful. There *is* a difference. Still, all *we* do is celebrate and congratulate ourselves on saving Europe from the infidel.

MÖHL: I know. . . . There's little credit for it.

HÖTZENDORF: Still. It *was* a long time ago.

MÖHL: Redl!

(*He hails* REDL *from the ballroom, who appears.*)
Redl, my dear boy! What a pleasant surprise. General, may I? Captain Alfred Redl: General Von Hötzendorf.
(*They acknowledge.*)
Since I last saw you, Redl, I now have the honour of working on the General's staff.

REDL: Indeed, sir. Congratulations.

MÖHL: Redl was just about the finest young officer, all round, when I was commandant in Lemberg, for eleven years.

HÖTZENDORF: So you told me. Who was the very pretty young lady you were dancing with?

REDL: I'm sorry, sir, which one?

MÖHL: Hah! Which *one!*

HÖTZENDORF: Small-boned, dark, brown eyes.

REDL: Miss Ursula Kunz, sir.

HÖTZENDORF: Kunz?

MÖHL: Ah, Kunz. Miss Kunz, youngest daughter of Judge Advocate Jaroslaw Kunz.

HÖTZENDORF: Ah.

MÖHL: Good man. Very.

HÖTZENDORF: Is he?

MÖHL: Seems to be.

HÖTZENDORF: Would you agree, Redl?

REDL: I, sir? From the little I know, and have been able to observe reliably, he is very competent indeed.

HÖTZENDORF: No more?

REDL: Accomplished, too . . . Unpopular.

HÖTZENDORF: Why?

REDL: I don't know, sir.

HÖTZENDORF: I believe it. Something odd, don't know what.

MÖHL: Well—yes . . . But how useful.

HÖTZENDORF: Oh, yes. Useful. Remember what Radetsky said about General Haynau? He said about Haynau, let's see: 'He's my best general all right, but he's like a razor. When you've used him, put him back in his case'.

MÖHL: The General was talking about Vienna, Redl. Well—— How are *you* enjoying it?

REDL: Very much, sir.

MÖHL: Better than St. Petersburg?

REDL: The Russians find it very difficult to enjoy life. Although they *do* manage occasionally.

HÖTZENDORF: Yes. Yes, but, you know, this is a great place to do *nothing*, sit in a café, and dream, listen

to the city, *do nothing* and not even anticipate
regretting it.

MÖHL: Ah, there's friend Kunz.

HÖTZENDORF: Who? Where?

MÖHL: With the Countess Delyanoff.

HÖTZENDORF: So he is.

MÖHL: You know her?

HÖTZENDORF: Just.

MÖHL: I think they're coming out here.

HÖTZENDORF: (*to* REDL). . . . Sort of woman, know
her——?

(REDL *shakes his head.*)

Well, the sort of woman who looks at you for five
minutes without a word and then says 'what do
you think about Shakespeare?' Or, something like
that. Unbelievable.

MÖHL: Ah, Kunz! Countess.

(*Enter* MAJOR JAROSLAW KUNZ *and the*
COUNTESS SOPHIA DELYANOFF.)

We were just watching you.

(MÖHL *makes the introductions, leaving* REDL *till last.*)

COUNTESS: We've met before.

REDL: Forgive me——

COUNTESS: Oh, yes. Not once, but at least three times.
You were on General Hauser's staff in St. Petersburg, and a short spell in Prague, were you not?

REDL: I'm sorry.

COUNTESS: Please. I'm sure you had no eye——

MÖHL: Oh, come, Countess, I can't think of anyone
more likely to get his eye fixed on someone like you.
You're being unfair.

COUNTESS: No. I think not. But I forgive him.

(*A* FLUNKEY *presents glasses of champagne.*)

MÖHL: The General and I were just talking about
Vienna.

KUNZ: Yes.

MÖHL: We were just saying—there's nowhere quite like it.

KUNZ: No. You've been away some time, I believe, Colonel. Where was it?

MÖHL: Przemysl.

KUNZ: Przemysl. Ah yes, with all the fortifications.

MÖHL: Four twelve-inch howitzers, some nine- and some six-inch, forty battalions, four squadrons, forty-three artillery companies, eight sapper companies —oh, please forgive me.

KUNZ: Yes. Nowhere quite like Przemysl, in fact.

COUNTESS: I'm afraid I simply can't understand the army, or why any man is ever in it.

HÖTZENDORF: Nor should you. The army's like nothing else. It goes beyond religion. It serves everyone and everyone serves it, even Hungarians and Jews. It conscripts, but it calls the best men out, men who'd never otherwise have been called on.

KUNZ: I think perhaps it's a little like living in the eighteenth century; the army. Apart from Przemysl, that is. Still that *is* a Viennese speciality? Don't you think, General?

HÖTZENDORF: I see nothing about the eighteenth century that makes me believe the nineteenth was any better. And what makes *you* think that the twentieth will be an improvement?

KUNZ: But why do you assume *I* should think it would be?

COUNTESS: I don't think I could ever have been a soldier. I'd want to be a stranger in a street, a key on a concierge's board, inaccessible if I wanted.

MÖHL: But that's what a *soldier* is.

COUNTESS: Only at the cost of his identity. Wouldn't you say, Captain? (*To* REDL.)

REDL: I think the General's right. The army creates an elite.

COUNTESS: No. I believe *it* is created. The army. It can't change. And it is changed from outside.

MÖHL: Nothing else trains a man——

48

KUNZ: Aptitudes, aptitudes at the expense of character.

COUNTESS: But it can, in its own way, provide a context of expression for people, who wouldn't otherwise have it.

KUNZ: I can only say, Countess, you can have met very few soldiers.

COUNTESS: You're quite wrong, Major. Why, look at me now. Several hundred guests and who am I with? The Chief of the General Staff himself, a distinguished Colonel from Przemysl, a Judge Advocate Major from Vienna and a splendid young Captain. And how different you all are, each one of you. I must say: I can't think of anything more admirable than not having to play a part.

KUNZ: I'm sorry, Countess, but nonsense! We all play parts, *are* doing so now, *will* continue to do so, and as long as we are playing at being Austrian, Viennese, or whatever we think we are, cosmopolitan and nondescript, a position palmed on us by history, by the accident of having held back the Muslim horde at the gates of Europe. For which no one is grateful, after all, it was two centuries ago, and we resent it, feel ill-used and pretend we're something we're not, instead of recognising that we're the provincial droppings of Europe. The Army, all of *us*, and the Church, sustain the Empire, which is what, a convenience to other nations, an international utility for the use of whoever, Russia, England or Francis Joseph, which again, is what? Crown Imperial of non-intellect. Which is why, for the moment, it survives. Like this evening, the Hofball, perspiring gaiety and pointlessness.

(*Pause.*)

HÖTZENDORF: Countess, please excuse me.

KUNZ: Plus a rather heavy odour of charm.

(HÖTZENDORF *clicks his heels and goes out.*)

COUNTESS: (*to* MÖHL). I'm sorry if I've offended the
General.

KUNZ: *I* offended, not you, Countess.

MÖHL: Correct. He's not accustomed to your kind of
young banter, Kunz.

KUNZ: I didn't expect him to take me so seriously.

COUNTESS: (*smiles*). Of course you did.

MÖHL: He is still the finest officer in the Royal and
Imperial Army.

KUNZ: Very probably.

MÖHL: He is an old friend. He may not be as clever as
you, Major, but his heart is in the right place.

KUNZ: Where it can be seen by everyone.

MÖHL: And I will not stand by and allow him to be
sneered at and insulted.

KUNZ: I quite agree. Please excuse me, Countess.
Gentlemen.

COUNTESS: Well. What tempers you men do have!
What about you, Captain, we've not heard much
out of you yet? I've a feeling you're full of shocking
things.

REDL: What about?

COUNTESS: Why, what we've been talking about.

REDL: Like the army, you mean? I'm afraid I don't
agree with the Major.

COUNTESS: No?

REDL: No. I mean, for myself, I didn't want to be, or
mean to be: rigid or fixed.

COUNTESS: But you're not.

REDL: No. At the same time, there must be bonds,
some bonds that have more meaning than others.

COUNTESS: I don't follow.

MÖHL: Now you're baiting, Countess. Of course he's
right. No officer should be allowed to speak in the
way of Major Kunz.

COUNTESS: He offends against blood. He——

MÖHL: Against himself; it's like being a Pole or a Slovak

or a Jew, I suppose. All these things have more
meaning than being, say, a civil servant, or a
watchmaker. And all these things are brought
together in the army like nowhere else. It's the
same experience as friendship or loving a woman,
speaking the same tongue, that is a *proper* bond,
it's *human*, you can see it and experience it, more
than 'all men are brothers' or some such nonsense.

COUNTESS: And do *you* agree with that, Captain Redl?

REDL: I don't agree that all men are brothers, like
Colonel Möhl. We are clearly not. Nor should be,
or ever want to be.

COUNTESS: Spoken like a true aristocrat.

REDL: Which, as you must know, I am not——

COUNTESS: Oh, but I believe you are. Don't you,
Colonel?

REDL: We're meant to clash. And often and violently. I
am proud to be despised by some men, no perhaps
most men. Others are to be tolerated or ignored.
And if they do the same for me, I am gratified, or,
at least, relieved.

MÖHL: I agree with the Countess about you, Redl. He
has style, always had it, must have had it as a tiny
boy.

COUNTESS: Your pride in the Captain is quite fierce,
Colonel. It's quite touching.

MÖHL: I don't know about touching, as you call it . . .
it's *real*, anyhow.

COUNTESS: But that's only too clear, and why not? It's
quite obviously justified.

MÖHL: Some men have a style of living like bad skins.
Coarse grained, erupting, spotty. Let me put it this
way: I don't have to tell you that, even in this
modern age of what they call democracy, the army
is still a place of privilege. Redl is the rare type
that redeems that privilege. And why? Because he
overpowers it, overpowers it by force, not mob-

51

trained force, but natural, disciplined character, ability and honour. And that's all I've got to say on the subject.

COUNTESS: My dear Colonel, I don't know who is the most embarrassed—you or Captain Redl.

REDL: Myself, Countess. A truly honest man is never embarrassed.

COUNTESS: You mean: *you* are not honest?

MÖHL: The boy's an open book. He should be in Intelligence. No one would believe him!

COUNTESS: But not tolerant.

REDL: I don't think so.

COUNTESS: Oh, indeed, I think you ignore what doesn't interest you. Which is why you didn't remember me in spite of the fact of our having met on three separate occasions.

REDL: Pardon me, Countess. I remembered immediately after.

COUNTESS: You think I am a snob because I accused you of trumpeting like an aristocrat just now. *You* are the snob, Captain Redl, not I. As Colonel Von Möhl here will tell you, my husband was a petty landowner from Cracow and *I* am the daughter of a veterinary surgeon.

MÖHL: (*laughs*). Well, don't take that too seriously, Redl.

COUNTESS: Colonel: I appeal to you!

MÖHL: Well, let me say you would say there was only *some* truth in it.

(*He chuckles again. A* FLUNKEY *approaches* REDL *with a salver with a card on it.*)

FLUNKEY: Captain Redl, sir?

REDL: Please excuse me.

(*He takes the card out of the envelope, reads it, hands it to* MÖHL.)

MÖHL: Archduke Ferdinand . . . Ah, well, you'd better get along! Quickly. Here, you!

(*Grabs more champagne glasses from passing* FLUNKEY.)

Get this down you first. Very beautiful, if I may
say so. Redl! Countess, your health. The Archduke's the man now. Ferdinand's the one to watch,
and I think he's probably all right. Knows what
he's doing. Knows what's going on in the Empire,
Hungary, for instance, Serbia. You see, the
Belvedere, that's going to be the centre of things,
not the Hofburg any more. Pity that, about all
that, what do you call it, morganatic marriage
business.

COUNTESS: Yes, indeed. Poor woman. Having to trail
behind countesses, a hundred yards behind him.

MÖHL: Why do you think he married her?

COUNTESS: Why does any man get married?

REDL: Children, property.

COUNTESS: But one sees all that, but it couldn't have
operated in this case. He could have had her
as his mistress like his uncle. But then, when you
think of the men one knows who *are* married, and
who they're married *to*, and what their real, snotty
little longings are underneath their proud watch
and chains, their constant broken, sidelong glances.
Oh, I know all about it, even if it's difficult to
understand sometimes. Captain, you mustn't keep
His Imperial Highness waiting. Not while *I* lecture
you on marriage.

(REDL *clicks his heels and leaves them.*)

MÖHL: Well!

COUNTESS: Yes, Colonel.

MÖHL: I was just thinking, what you were saying about
marriage then.

COUNTESS: And——?

MÖHL: It really is the most *lamentable* thing for most of
us, isn't it? I mean, as you say, it doesn't work
really. Only the appearances function. Eh?
Everyone knows the *feelings*, but what's the answer,
what's the answer do you think?

53

COUNTESS: The only answer is not to be drawn into it, like the Captain.

MÖHL: No, I think you're wrong there. Redl would make a first-class husband.

COUNTESS: You think so?

MÖHL: Absolutely. He's steadfast, sober, industrious, orderly, he likes orderly things, hates chaos. That's why marriage would suit him so well. That's what marriage represents, I suppose. I say, I *am* enjoying talking to you.

COUNTESS: And I am enjoying talking to you. Do you think Captain Redl will come back to us?

MÖHL: Oh, I should think so. Order out of chaos. I know, we'll keep an eye out for him, learn what the Archduke had to say to him. You wouldn't care to dance with such an old man, would you?

COUNTESS: But, of course, delighted. Major Kunz is a very uninspired dancer.

MÖHL: That's because he dosen't like it. Now *I* love it. I'm so glad Redl got that invitation. Good boy! Oh, I say, I *am* having a good time.

(*He beams boyishly, offers his arm to her, and they leave the terrace to join the dancers in the ballroom.*)

FADE

54

Scene 7

One drawing room of COUNTESS DELYANOFF'S *house. One oil lamp burns on a desk. On a chair are* REDL'S *tunic, sword, and cap and gloves. A sharp, clear, moaning cry is heard. Once, quickly. Then again, longer, more violent. Then silence. Fumbling footsteps outside the door.* REDL *enters in his breeches, putting on his vest, carrying his boots. He slumps into a chair, dropping the boots beside him. A voice outside calls softly: 'Alfred, Alfred!'*

The COUNTESS *enters swiftly, anxious, her hair down to her waist, very beautiful in her nightgown. She looks across at* REDL *as if this had happened before, goes to a decanter and pours a brandy. With it, she crosses to* REDL'S *armchair and looks down at him.*

REDL: Sophia?

COUNTESS: My dear?

REDL: Sorry I woke you.

COUNTESS: I should think you woke the entire street.

REDL: Sorry. So sorry.

COUNTESS: Don't be silly. Here.

> *(She hands him the brandy. He takes some. Stares at his boots.)*

REDL: I think I'd better go.

COUNTESS: It's early yet. Why, it's only, I can't see, look, it's only half-past one.

REDL: Still . . .

COUNTESS: You left me *last* night at three. And when you're gone I can't sleep. I wake the moment you've gone. All I can do is think about you.

REDL: I know. Please forgive me. . . . Better put these on.

55

(*Takes one of the boots.*)

COUNTESS: Alfred. Please come back to bed. . . . I know you hate me asking you, but I do beg you. . . . Just for an hour. You *can't* go out now.

REDL: I need some air.

COUNTLESS: (*softly*) Darling—

REDL: Need my orderly on these occasions. Can't get my boots on.

(*She grasps his knee and kneels.*)

COUNTESS: Why did you wake?

REDL: Oh: Usual.

COUNTESS: And you're crying again.

REDL: I know. . . . (*His face is stony. His voice firm.*) Why do you always have to look at me?

COUNTESS: Because I love you.

REDL: You'd look away . . .

COUNTESS: That's why. What can I do, my darling?

REDL: Nothing. . . . I must get these damned things . . . (*Struggles with boots*). I'd love another brandy.

(*She rises and gets it.*)

It's like a disease.

COUNTESS: What is?

REDL: Oh, all this incessant, *silly* weeping. It only happens, it creeps up on me, when I'm asleep. No one else has ever noticed it. . . . Why do you have to wake up?

COUNTESS: Here. Alfred: don't turn away from me.

REDL: My mouth tastes sour.

COUNTESS: I didn't mean that. Anyway, what if it is? Don't turn your head away.

(*She grasps his head and kisses him. He submits for a moment, then thrusts her away.*)

REDL: Please!

COUNTESS: What is it? Me?

REDL: No. You're—you're easily the most beautiful . . . desirable woman I've ever . . . There couldn't be . . .

56

COUNTESS: It's not easy to believe.

REDL: Sophia: it's *me*. It's like a disease.

COUNTESS: You must feel deeply. So do I. Why do you
think you've got *me* crying as well. No one's done
that to me for years!

REDL: It's like, I can't . . .

COUNTESS: (*impatient*). But it *isn't* like the clap you got
off some garrison whore. That's all over. You know
it, you were cured, cured, you've got a paper to say
so, and even if you weren't do you think I would care?

REDL: It isn't that.

COUNTESS: Then what is it? Why do you dream? Why
do you sweat and cry out and *leave* me in the
middle of the night? Oh, God!
(*She recovers.*)

REDL: Here, have some of this. I'll get some more.

COUNTESS: No, that's fine.

REDL: Why don't you commit yourself?

COUNTESS: Why don't *you*? My darling, try not to drink
so much.

REDL: I've told you. I drink. I drink, heavily sometimes, I don't get *drunk*.

COUNTESS: Yes. So you say.

REDL: It's the truth.

COUNTESS: What are you saying? No, forget I asked.
Don't take any of this as *true*, Alfred, I beg of you.
It's early in the morning, everything's asleep and
indifferent now—*threatening to us*, both of us, *you're*
in tears, you wake up in a depression, in a panic,
you're dangerous and frightened again and I'm in
tears. Please, don't, please, stay, stay with me, I'll
look after you, I'll make up . . . at least for
something. I'll protect you, protect you . . . and
love you.

REDL: I can protect myself.

COUNTESS: But you can't. Not *always*. Can you? What
is it?

57

REDL: I must go. I can't sit here.

COUNTESS: Why can't you trust me?

REDL: I've told you . . . I *don't* mean to hurt you.

COUNTESS: And I believe you.

REDL: I just can't.

(*Pause.*)

COUNTESS: Have you never confided in anyone?

REDL: No.

COUNTESS: Hasn't there ever been anyone? (*Pause.*)
What about another man? I know friendship means
a lot to you. . . . What about Taussig?

REDL: No. At least . . . Only a very, a very little. I did
try one evening. But he doesn't welcome con-
fidences. He doesn't know what to do with them
. . . or where to put them.

COUNTESS: You mean nobody else, not *one*, your mother,
your grandfather, no one?

REDL: They might have been;——

COUNTESS: Um?

REDL: But I never did.

COUNTESS: Why?

REDL: I suppose I . . . they, *I* waited too long, and then
. . . they were killed. An accident. You're
shivering.

COUNTESS: Please try. Everyone owes something to
someone. You *are* in love with me, Alfred, I know
you are, and you've told me yourself. That must be
something.

REDL: Put this on.

(*He places his tunic round her shoulders.*)

COUNTESS: What about you?

(*He shrugs.*)

You look better. *Are* you?

REDL: Yes. At least they go quickly. Just at a bad time.
In the night. Or when I'm having to force myself
to do something as an exercise, or a duty, like
working late.

58

COUNTESS: I tell you: you work too hard.

REDL: Or sometimes I get caught in some relaxation. Sitting in a café, listening to gossip, and I enjoy that after a long day, and I'm curious. But if I listen to a conversation that's got serious, say, about politics, the Magyars or merging with Germany, or something like that, I feel myself, almost as if I were falling away and disappearing. I want to run. . . . But, I've felt I should take a serious, applied interest in this sort, in, ours is a complicated age, and I'm some small part of it, and I should devote as much attention and interest to it as I can muster. I should be giving up time—

COUNTESS: What time, for heaven's sake? You already——

REDL: Much more than I do, *much* more. I used not even to try.

COUNTESS: You mean *I* waste it?

REDL: But I can't relax or be at ease.

COUNTESS: Why are you so watchful? You always seem to be at the ready in some way, listening for something . . . some stray chance thing.

REDL: I don't know what that means.

(*He goes to the decanter.*)

COUNTESS: Please, Alfred. You've an early train in the morning . . .

REDL: Do you know: the only time I drink heavily is when I'm with you? No, I didn't mean that. But when you're badgering me and sitting on my head and, and I can't breathe.

COUNTESS: Why do you always have to make love to me with the——

REDL: There you go!

COUNTESS: Why? Why do you insist? Before we even begin?

REDL: I might ask you why *you* insist on turning the light on.

COUNTESS: Because I want to look at your face. Is that so strange?

REDL: You must know, *you* must know, we're not all the same.

COUNTESS: Why do you never kiss me?

REDL: But I do.

COUNTESS: But never in bed.

REDL: Oh, let's go back. We're tired.

COUNTESS: And turn your head away?

REDL: Damn your eyes, I *won't* be catechized!

COUNTESS: Why do you never speak?

REDL: What do you want out of me? Well, I tell you, whatever it is, I *can't* give it. Can't and won't. (*Pause.*)

COUNTESS: I thought it was only whores you didn't kiss or speak to.

REDL: You would know more about that.
(*She looks up at him miserably, shivering. He feels out-manoeuvred. Takes his tunic from her and puts it on.*)
Excuse me.

COUNTESS: If you leave me, you'll be alone.

REDL: That's what I want, to be left alone.

COUNTESS: You'll always be alone.

REDL: Good. Splendid.

COUNTESS: No it isn't. You know it isn't. That's why you're so frightened. You'll fall alone.

REDL: So does everyone. Even if they don't know it.

COUNTESS: You can't be *saved* alone.

REDL: I don't expect to be saved, as you put it. Not by you.

COUNTESS: Or any other woman?

REDL: Or anyone at all.
(*He picks up his cap and gloves.*)

COUNTESS: What have I done?

REDL: *I* am the guilty one. Not you. Please forgive me.

COUNTESS: Don't, don't go. (*Pause.*) One feels very old at this time of night.

(She goes to the window. He watches her, distressed.)
It's the time of night when people die. People give up.
(He goes behind her, hesitates, puts his head against hers for comfort. Pause.)
You can't have your kind of competitive success *and* seclusion.
(He sighs, draws away and goes to the door.)

REDL: Good night, Sophia.

COUNTESS: Good night.

(Pause.)

REDL: Would you like to have tea?

COUNTESS: When?

REDL: Tuesday?

COUNTESS: I can't.

REDL: Wednesday?

COUNTESS: Please.

(He turns.)
Yes, please.
(He goes out.)

FADE

Scene 8

OBLENSKY's *office. He is reading a letter to* STANITSIN.

OBLENSKY: 'In haste. Enroute for Prague. Wherever I
am, my dearest, you will trouble my heart. I can
say no more, I cannot think. The work here will do
me good I expect. Try to do something yourself.
This is a difficult time. I seem to: seem to——'
can't read it—'speak . . . speak out of nowhere. You
deserve only the best, not the worst. Forgive me:
Alfred'. Where's hers? Ah: 'My dearest love, why
are you writing to me like this? You seem to have
forgotten everything. It was not all like those short
times during the night. The rest *was* different'—
underlined. 'Don't, I beg you, *don't* deceive yourself. Why don't you answer my letters? I wait for
them. Give me a word, or something that will do.
At least something I can go over. I can do
nothing. Now *I* am helpless. Loved one, don't
something this. Forever, your Sophia. P.S. Did you
never intend coming that Wednesday? I can't
believe it.' Hum. What do you suppose he means,
where is it—'this is a difficult time'?

STANITSIN: Well, the moneylenders are pressing pretty
hard. He's sold his gold cigarette case and fancy
watch.

OBLENSKY: Has he? 'You deserve only the best, not the
worst.' Odd sentiment for a distinguished officer,
don't you think? He can't feel *that* sensitive about
his extravagance, he's too reckless. Besides, as far as
he knows, she's quite rich.

STANITSIN: Maybe he's just bored with her.

OBLENSKY: I don't think so, I'd say he's a passionate
man, a bit callous too, and selfish, very, but there's
something *in* all this.

STANITSIN: Come to that, the Countess sounds pretty
convincing.

OBLENSKY: I hope not. All right.

(*He nods to* STANITSIN, *who opens the office door, and
admits the* COUNTESS.)

Sit down. You seem to have lost your man.

COUNTESS: For the moment.

OBLENSKY: You mean you think you can get him back?

COUNTESS: Possibly.

OBLENSKY: Do you want to?

COUNTESS: What do you mean? I do what you tell me.

OBLENSKY: What's your assessment of Redl?

COUNTESS: Ambitious. Secretive. Violent. Vain.
Extravagant. I expect you know as much as I do.
You don't have to sleep with him to find that out.

OBLENSKY: Precisely. It doesn't seem to have added
much to our total knowledge. However, patience.
We're in no hurry. Captain Redl will be with us for
a long time yet. Years and years. He'll probably
improve with keeping. What's he doing with
himself?

STANITSIN: What he says, working. Of course, he's hard
up for the moment, but he'll——

OBLENSKY: Have you offered him money?

COUNTESS: Twice. He refused.

OBLENSKY: Won't take money from a woman. And I
suppose you told him it didn't count between
lovers?

COUNTESS: Naturally.

OBLENSKY: And there's no woman in Prague, nowhere,
anyone? No one night stands or twopenny stand-
ups?

STANITSIN: Nothing. He leaves his office in the War

Building every day at 4.15, goes down to the café, has a coffee or two, reads all the foreign newspapers, has an early dinner, then goes back to his office and works till about ten, even eleven or twelve sometimes.

OBLENSKY: He *is* telling the truth.

STANITSIN: Occasionally he'll drop in for a drink somewhere on his way home or meets his friend Taussig for half an hour. More often than not he just sits alone.

OBLENSKY: Doing nothing?

STANITSIN: Just sitting. Looking.

OBLENSKY: Looking at what?

STANITSIN: I don't know. What *can* you look at from a café window? Other people, I suppose. Watch.

OBLENSKY: The Passing Show.

COUNTESS: Is there anything else?

OBLENSKY: No, my dear. Stanitsin will brief you.
(*She rises.*)

COUNTESS: Is it—may I have my letter?

OBLENSKY: I don't see why not.
(*Hands one to her.*)

COUNTESS: No, I meant his, to me.

OBLENSKY: I'm afraid that's for the File. Sorry. I can send you a copy. I wonder if he *will* write again. Don't forget to report, will you?
(STANITSIN *sees her out.* OBLENSKY *lights a cigarette.*)

FADE

Scene 9

A café. REDL *sits alone at a table. Sitting a few tables away is a young man.* REDL *reads a paper. Throws away his cigar butt. Enter* TAUSSIG.

TAUSSIG: Ah, Redl, there you are. Sorry I'm late.

REDL: What will you have?

TAUSSIG: Don't think I'll bother. I promised to meet someone in ten minutes.

REDL: The one in the chorus at the Opera House?

TAUSSIG: That's the one.

REDL: Where?

TAUSSIG: She's taking me to her lodgings.

REDL: Before the performance? I hope it doesn't affect her voice. What's she like?

TAUSSIG: She rattles. Nice big girl.

REDL: They always are.

TAUSSIG: She's got a girl friend.

REDL: Thank you, no.

TAUSSIG: You seem awfully snobbish sometimes, Alfred.

REDL: Do I? I'm sorry. It's just that I'm not too keen on the opera. Are you going—afterwards?

TAUSSIG: What?

REDL: To the performance?

TAUSSIG: Oh, yes, I suppose so. Your head must be hardened by all those ciphers. Löhengrin, I think. What's it like?

REDL: Boring.

TAUSSIG: So I believe. Oh, well. Sure you won't have

65

supper after? She really is quite nice. They both
are.

REDL: No, thank you, really.

TAUSSIG: Not going to Madame Heyse's do are you?

REDL: No. (*Pause.*)

TAUSSIG: Does that young man over there know you?

REDL: What young man?

TAUSSIG: Well, there's only one.

REDL: No. Why?

TAUSSIG: He's done nothing but stare at you. Oh, he's
turned away now. Knows we're talking about him.

REDL: Prague's as bad as Vienna.

TAUSSIG: Keeps giggling to himself, as far as I can see.

REDL: Probably a cretin. Or a Czech who hates
Austrian Army officers. I can't face another of those
evenings or dinners, here or anywhere. They all talk
about each other. They're all clever and they're
afraid of each other's cleverness. They're like
beautiful, schooled performing dogs. Scrutinizing
and listening for an unsteady foot. It's like hunting
without the pig. Everyone sweats and whoops and
rides together, and, at any time, at any moment,
the pig may turn out to be *you*. Stick!

TAUSSIG: Well, if I can't tempt you . . . Can I have one
of your cigarettes? I say, the old case back, eh?

REDL: And the watch, Everything in fact.

TAUSSIG: Good for you. Make a killing?

REDL: I tipped my mare against Steinbauer's new
gelding. Want a loan?

TAUSSIG: No thanks. The Countess isn't bothering you,
is she?

REDL: I told you—no. We never got on. She was
prickly and we were always awkward together. It
was like talking to my sister. Who died, last week
incidentally, consumption, and I can't say I
thought about it more than ten minutes.

TAUSSIG: What will you do?

66

REDL: Now? Oh, have a quiet dinner. Go for a walk.

TAUSSIG: A walk? I don't know—well, if I can't persuade you. 'Bye.

(REDL *nods.* TAUSSIG *strides off. He picks up a paper, lights a new cigar. Presently the* YOUNG MAN *comes up to him.*)

YOUNG MAN: Excuse me, sir.

REDL: Well?

YOUNG MAN: May I glance at your paper?

REDL: If you wish. (*Irritated.*) The waiter will bring you one if you ask.

YOUNG MAN: I only want to see what's on at the Opera.

REDL: Löhengrin.

YOUNG MAN: Oh, thank you. No. I don't think I like Wagner much. Do you?

REDL: No. Now please go away.

(*The* YOUNG MAN *grins at him, and leans across to him, saying softly.*)

YOUNG MAN: I know what *you're* looking for.

(REDL *looks stricken. The* YOUNG MAN *walks away. He is almost out of sight when* REDL *runs after him.*)

REDL: You!

(REDL *grabs him with ferocious power by the neck.*)
What do you mean?

YOUNG MAN: Nothing! Let me go!

REDL: You pig, you little upstart pig. What did you mean?

YOUNG MAN: (*yells*). Let me go!

(*Heads turn.* REDL's *anger subsides into embarrassment. The* YOUNG MAN *walks away.* REDL *returns to his seat, lights his cigar, orders a drink from the* WAITER. *A Gipsy Band strikes up.*)

FADE

67

Scene 10

A bare, darkened room. In it is a bed. On it two figures, not yet identifiable. A light is struck. A cigar end glows.

REDL'S VOICE: Why wouldn't you keep the light on?
  (*A figure leaves the bed and goes to a wash basin. Sound of water.*)
  Um? Oh! Why did I wait—so long.
  (REDL *lights a lamp beside the bed. By the washstand is the handsome form of a young* PRIVATE SOLDIER.)
  Paul?
PAUL: Yes?
REDL: Why?
PAUL: I don't know. I just prefer the dark.
REDL: But why? My darling. You're so exquisite to look on—— You mean it's me?
PAUL: No. You look all right.
REDL: What is it, then? What are you dressing for?
PAUL: Got to get back to barracks, haven't I?
REDL: What's your unit?
PAUL: That'd be telling, wouldn't it?
REDL: Oh, come on, I can find out.
PAUL: Yes. General Staff and all that, isn't it?
REDL: Paul. What is it? What have I done? What are you opening the door for?
  (PAUL *has opened the door. Four young* SOLDIERS *come in. They look at* REDL, *who knows instantly what will happen. He struggles violently at first, and for a while it looks as if they might have taken on too much. The young* SOLDIERS *in turn become amazed by* REDL'S *vicious*

68

defence of himself, which is like an attack. All the while
PAUL *dresses, pockets* REDL'S *gold cigarette case, cigar case, watch and chain, gold crucifix, notes and change.*
REDL *becomes a kicked, bloody heap on the floor. The*
SOLDIERS *leave.* PAUL, *having dressed fully by now, helps* REDL *sit up against the bed, looks down at his bloody face.*

PAUL: Don't be too upset, love. You'll get used to it.
　　Exit.

CURTAIN

END OF ACT I

ACT II *Scene 1*

A Ballroom, Vienna. A winter evening in 1902. In the background a small, eccentrically dressed ORCHESTRA *plays. The light is not bright when the curtain goes up, except on the* SINGERS. *Concentrated silently, at first, anyway, are the* GUESTS, *among whom is* REDL, *one of the few not in fancy dress of some kind. However, he looks magnificent in his uniform and has put on his few decorations. He sprawls, listening thoughtfully to the* SINGER, *smoking one of his long black cigars. The* SINGER *is dressed in an eighteenth century dress which might allow the wearer to play Susanna in 'Figaro' or one of Mozart's ladies like* ZERLINA. *The* ORCHESTRA *plays very softly, the* SINGER *is restrained at this time, which is as well, because the voice is not adequate. However, it has enough sweetness in feeling to immediately invoke the pang of Mozart. Perhaps 'Vedrai Carino' or 'Batti, Batti' from 'Don Giovanni'. It ends quickly. Applause. Then a* MAN *dressed to play 'Figaro' appears, the lights become brighter, and the two go into the duet in the first scene of 'Figaro'. This should take no more than three minutes. It should be accepted at the beginning as the indifferent effort of a court opera house cast with amateurs, but not without charm and aplomb.*

The 'Figaro' in this case is a straight man. Presently, the 'Susanna' begins straight, then gradually cavorting, camping, and sending up the character, the audience, and Mozart as only someone in drag has the licence. The ballroom audience has been waiting for this, and is in ecstasy by the time it is over. Some call out 'do the Mad Scene'. Or 'Come Scoglio'. The 'Susanna', egged on, does a short parody of something like 'Come Scoglio', or 'Lucia' done in the headlong, take-it-on-the-chin manner.

This only takes a couple of minutes and should be quite funny. Anyhow, the ballroom audience apparently think so. Obviously, most of them have seen the performance before. There is a lot of giggling and even one scream during the ARIA, *which 'Susanna-Lucia' freezes with mock fury, and ends to great applause. 'Susanna' curtsies graciously. The lights in the room come up, the* ORCHESTRA *strikes up and most of the guests dance. It is essential that it should only gradually be revealed to the audience that all the dancers and guests are men. The costumes, from all periods, should be in exquisite taste, both men's and women's, and those wearing them should look exotic and reasonably attractive, apart from an occasional grotesque. The music is gay, everyone chatters happily like a lot of birds and the atmosphere is generally relaxed and informal, in contrast to the somewhat stiff atmosphere at the ball in Act I. Among those dancing at present are* KUPFER, *dressed rather dashingly as* SCARAMOUCHE. KUNZ, *dancing one handed, with* MARIE ANTOINETTE, *looks rather good as* LORD NELSON. *The* WAITER ALBRECHT *from Scene 3, dressed as* COLUMBINE *with* KUPFER. FIGARO *dances with a* LADY GODIVA *in gold lamé jockstrap.* DOWNSTAGE, *holding court, is the host,* BARON VON EPP. *He is an imposing man with a rich flexible voice which he uses to effect. At present, he looks astonishingly striking with upswept hair, ospreys in pompadour feathers, a pearl and diamond dog collar at his neck, and a beautiful fan, as* QUEEN ALEXANDRA. *Again, it is essential that the costume should be in meticulous taste and worn elegantly and with natural confidence. Sitting beside him is someone dressed as a whimpled mediaeval lady, to be identified as* STEINBAUER. *Like* REDL *now, some years older.* REDL *is accompanied by* LIEUTENANT STEFAN KOVACS, *who is fixed in a mixture of amusement and embarrassment.* REDL *himself is quite cool, looking extremely dashing in his Colonel's uniform and decorations and close-cropped hair, staring very carefully around at all the guests, his eyes missing no one. He lights one of his long black cigars and joins the* BARON's *group, which includes* STEINBAUER, SUSANNA *and a ravishing* TSARINA.

72

NOTE: At any drag ball as stylish and private as this one the guests can be seen to belong to entirely different and very distinct categories.

1. The paid bum boys whose annual occasion it is—they wait for it from one year to the next and spend between 3 and 6 months preparing an elaborate and possibly bizarre costume. This is the market place where in all probability they will manage to acquire a meal ticket for months ahead. They tend to either tremendously careful, totally feminine clothes—or the ultimate in revelation— e.g. Lady Godiva, except that he/she might think, instead of a gold lamé jockstrap, that a gold chastity belt with a large and obvious gold key on a chain round her/his neck, be better.

2. The discreet drag queens. Like the Baron/Queen Alexandra, and the Tsarina—their clothes, specially made for the occasion by a trusted dressmaker, as the night becomes wilder are usually found to have a removable skirt revealing stockings, suspenders, jewelled garters and diamond buckles on their shoes. But even despite this mild strip tease, they still remain in absolutely perfect taste.

3. The more self-conscious rich queens, who, though in drag, tend to masculine drag, and end up looking like lesbians. Someone tells me they saw one once in marvellously cut black riding habit—frilled white jabot and cuffs—long skirt and boots—top hat with veil. Also in this category are the ones who go out of their way to turn themselves into absolute grotesques, and quite often arrive in a gaggle. They make a regal entry enjoying having their disguise penetrated or not as the case may be. If, for instance, the theme of the ball were theatrical they would probably chose to come as the witches from Macbeth. But marvellously theatrically thought out in every detail.

4. Another category of rich, discreet queens, who don't want to offend their host by making no effort at all but

73

who baulk at dressing up; for them full and impeccable evening dress with sash orders and neck decorations and elaborately over made-up faces. They usually look more frightening than any of the others—with middle-aged decadent faces, painted like whores.

5. There are the men who positively dislike women and only put on drag in order to traduce them and make them appear as odious, immoral and unattractive as possible.

6. Finally, the ones who don't even make that effort but wear, like Redl, full-dress uniform and decorations—or evening dress.

It's not inconceivable that some of the bum boys would dress as pampered children.

Remember when they dance you don't find the male ones only dancing with the female ones—but possibly a hussar with a man in evening dress—or two men in evening dress together—or two shepherdesses together.

In category 4 you would also be likely to find the made-up face—the impeccable tails and white tie plus ropes of pearls and blazing diamonds.

BARON: Ah, Redl! How good to see you. Where have you been? You're always so busy. Everyone says you're in Counter Intelligence or something and you're frightfully grand now. I hope you're not spying on anyone here, Colonel. You know I won't have that sort of thing. I only give this ball once a year, and everyone invited is under the obligation of strictest confidence. No gossiping after. Otherwise you can all do as you like. Who's this?

REDL: May I introduce Lieutenant Stefan Kovacs— Baron Von Epp.

BARON: Very nice. Why are you both in mufti? You know my rule.

REDL: I wouldn't call the dress uniform of the Royal Imperial Army exactly mufti.

BARON: I'm surprised they let you in. I expect you know everyone, or will do.

74

REDL: It's rather astonishing. Almost everyone.

BARON: It's not astonishing at all. Colonel Redl, this is Captain Steinbauer—aren't you? Yes. She is.

REDL (*to* STEINBAUER). Lemberg. Seventh Galician.

STEINBAUER: That's right. Siczynski.

REDL: Yes.

> (*They look at each other. Sudden gratitude for the remembrance. And weariness, sadness. The* BARON *quickly dismisses the cloud.*)

BARON: And that's the Tsarina there. I don't know *who* she is exactly. A Russian spy I should think. Watch yourself, my dear, the Colonel eats a spy in bed every morning, don't you, Alfred? That's what they all tell me. It's even in the papers. And this is Ferdy.

> (*He indicates* SUSANNA.)

Didn't you think he was divine?

REDL: Superb.

STEFAN: He really has a fine voice. I thought he was a real soprano at first.

> (*They all look at him with some suspicion.*)

SUSANNA: What do you mean? I *am* a real soprano!

> (*They all laugh.* STEFAN *feels he has blundered more than he has in fact.* REDL *chips in.*)

REDL: Isn't that Major Advocate Kunz?

BARON: Where? Oh, yes I see. Nelson, you mean. Doesn't he look marvellous. One arm and all! Wonder where he keeps it? He's my insurance.

REDL: What?

BARON: If there's ever any trouble, Kunz is my legal insurance. *Very* influential that one! She'll deal with anything that ever came up—Secret Police, anything, spies. No, spies is you, isn't it, Alfred, *you're* the spy-catcher, we'll leave any lovely little spies to you. (*To* TSARINA.) Wait till he catches *you*. I daren't think *what* he'll do to you!

> (*The* TSARINA *giggles.*)

Eh, Alfred? What do you do to naughty little spies?

REDL: (*bends down and grasps the* TSARINA's *ear lobe*). I tie them over the back of my mare, Kristina, on a leading rein, and beat them with my crop at a slow canter.

BARON: How delicious! Now, her earring's fallen off, you've excited her so!

(*The* TSARINA *retrieves her earring and smiles up in a sweet, friendly curious way at* REDL, *who smiles back, touched by an instant, simple, affectionate spirit. He turns to* STEFAN, *who has looked away. Quickly noted by the* BARON.)

BARON: I haven't seen your Lieutenant Kovacs before, Alfred.

REDL: He's only just graduated from the War School.

BARON: All that studying and hardening the body and noontide heat and sweating, and horses! You all look quite beautiful, well, some of you, but I hate to think of you in a war. A real war.

(*A* SHEPHERDESS *serves champagne*.)

Oh, come along, come along. No one's drinking half enough yet. Alfred!

(REDL *downs a glass. He looks flushed and suddenly relaxed*.)

And another! You're behind the rest of us. And a good place for you, said someone.

(REDL *takes another. Hands one to* STEFAN.)

And Ferdy, you have some more. Good for the voice. Bit strained tonight, dear. I want you to do 'Una Donna A Quindici Anna'.

FERDY: Don't think I can.

BARON: You can do *anything*. Practically. (*To* REDL.) He has hair on his instep—like a goat. Show them. Oh, well . . . Where have you two come from? The Lieutenant looks rather glum.

REDL: We were at the Hofburg for an hour or two.

76

BARON: No wonder he looks glum. Come along! Drink up, Lieutenant. I can't have anyone sober at my party. (*To* REDL.) I suppose you *had* to go, being so powerful now and impressive.

REDL: Oh, come along.

BARON: No, I hear it's quite true. (*To* STEINBAUER.) You remember the Colonel then?

STEINBAUER: Years ago. I always knew he'd make a brilliant officer. We all did. Congratulations, Colonel! (*Raises glass—talks to* TSARINA.)

BARON: Mind your wimple. She gets drunk too easily, that one. Which is probably why she's still only a humble captain in number seventy-seven. (*Out of* STEFAN's *hearing.*) Are you sure your friend wouldn't rather be back at the Hofburg?

REDL: He'll be all right. Try and leave him alone.

BARON: I can't leave anyone *that* pretty alone. Do you want the Tsarina? She's Kunz's really, but she's pretty available. (*Pause.* REDL *considers.*) And Kunz isn't the kind who makes scenes. He doesn't care ... He's a bit cold too.

(STEFAN *hears the last of this.*)

STEFAN: Did you say Kunz? Isn't a man like that taking a bit of a risk?

BARON: Aren't we all?

STEFAN: Yes, but for someone ...

BARON: We are none of us safe. This——

(*He sweeps his fan round the ballroom.*)

is the celebration of the individual against the rest, the us's and the them's, the free and the constricted, the gay and the dreary, the lonely and the mob, the little Tsarina there and the Emperor Francis Joseph.

(*They laugh.*)

Tell your friend it's so, Alfred.

REDL: Oh, I agree.

STEFAN: (*To* REDL.) Forgive me, I feel I'm unwanted.

77

BARON: Nonsense. You're *wanted*. Tell him not to be a
silly, solemn boy, Alfred.
(REDL *squeezes the boy's arm and laughs. The* BARON
refills STEFAN'S *glass.*)
Actually, Kunz is an odd one. He seems to take
appalling risks, but he knows the right people
everywhere and anywhere, and he'd sell anyone,
and I know him. He's my first cousin. He'd do it
to me.
STEFAN: Blood not thicker than water?
BARON: His blood is thinner than anything, my dear.
FERDY: Darling! She wants to know——
BARON: What is it? I'm talking.
FERDY: Are you really a Baron?
(*The* TSARINA *giggles.*)
BARON: Tell her she'll find out if she's not careful.
TSARINA: (*to* FERDY). Are you the Baroness then?
FERDY: (*nods*). Oh. I let him. He fancies himself chasing
the ladies, but he's just the same as I am. Nothing
more at all.
TSARINA: What about the Lieutenant?
FERDY: Oh, I should think so. Either too stupid to
know it, or hasn't woken up to it yet.
TSARINA: Or doesn't want to wake up to it. Looks a bit
dreary.
FERDY: Do you fancy him? You'll have the Colonel
after you. You'll be shot down.
(*While this duet has gone on, the* BARON, STEFAN *and*
REDL *have drawn away from the* GIRLS *into their own
conversation. Some class division here too.*)
BARON: Vienna is so dull! All that Spanish gloom at the
Hofburg gets in everywhere, like the moth.
FERDY: (*calls out*). *You* need moth balls! (*Collapse.*)
BARON: The Viennese gull themselves they're gay, but
they're just stiff-jointed aristocrats like puppets,
grubbing little tradesmen or Jews and chamber-
maids making a lot of one-two-three noises all the

78

time. Secretly, they're feeling utterly thwarted and empty. The bourgeoisie daren't enjoy themselves except at someone else's expense or misfortune. And all those cavorting, clever Jews are even more depressing, pretending to be generous—and *entirely* unspontaneous. Hungarians, they're gay, perhaps that's because they're quite selfish and pig-headed. Kovacs: oh, dear, are you Hungarian? Well, never mind, that's me again I'm afraid, speak first, think afterwards——

REDL: No, Baron, you're ahead of everyone.

BARON: Only wish I were. Poles are fairly gay. You're Polish or something, aren't you, Alfred? And somehow they're less *common* than Russians. Serbs are impossible, of course, savage, untrustworthy, worse than Hungarians, infidels in every sense. I think your friend despises me because I'm such a snob. What is your father, Lieutenant?

STEFAN: A chef at the Volksgarten Restaurant.

BARON: And do you think I'm a snob?

STEFAN: You appear to be.

BARON: Well, of course, I am. Alfred will tell you how much. However, I'm also a gentleman, which is preferable to being one of our dear Burgomaster Lueger's mob. Taste, a silk shirt, a perfumed hand, an ancient Greek ring are things that come from a way not only of thinking but of being. They can add up to a man. (*To* STEFAN.) Would you like to walk on the terrace? The view is rather remarkable on an evening like this.

STEFAN: Alfred?

BARON: We'll join you. Or come back soon. I want to ask the Colonel's advice. About some espionage. (STEFAN *bows and leaves through the high central glass doors.*)·
Well, my dear friend. And how are you? You're prosperous I hear.

79

REDL: I had a small legacy.

BARON: Good. A man like you knows what money's for. And you *look* so well. Forgive me for sending the boy away for a moment.

REDL: That's all right. He'll find something to amuse him.

BARON: Would it be impertinent to ask: you're not wasting your time there are you?

REDL: It would.

BARON: What? Oh, I see. Quite right. Only I admire you, Redl. So does everyone else. You're a credit to—everyone. I just want you to succeed in everything you undertake.

REDL: Thank you.

(KUNZ *comes over with his partner,* MARIE ANTOIN-ETTE.)

BARON: Jaroslaw! Have some champagne.

KUNZ: Thank you.

BARON: And let me introduce Colonel Redl—Major Advocate Kunz.

(*They salute each other appropriately.*)

FERDY: Colonel! Would you come over here a minute. The Tsarina wants to give herself up.

(TSARINA *screams.*)

She says, she says she wants to confess!

(*The* TSARINA *pulls off* FERDY's *wig and smacks him with it.* REDL *smiles and excuses himself to* KUNZ.)

BARON: Ferdy! That's naughty! The Colonel was talking to Major Kunz.

FERDY: No, he wasn't. Here!

(*He places* REDL *beside him and the* TSARINA.)

We've been talking to you. (*To* BARON.) *You* don't listen! It's secret.

(*The* BARON *smiles happily.*)

BARON: Alfred *knows* all the secrets. It's his job.

(FERDY *and the* TSARINA *conduct a whispered conversation with* REDL *for a while. He is drinking freely now,*

and is excited and enjoying himself. The BARON *turns to*
KUNZ.)
Don't you think my little Ferdy's brilliant? He'd
make an adorable 'Cherubino'.

KUNZ: I think he's prettier as 'Susanna'.

BARON: Perhaps. He made that costume himself. Up
half the night.

KUNZ: Did you see who I came with?

BARON: No. Why?

KUNZ: Good. I thought I'd spice your party a bit this
year.

BARON: What have you done?

KUNZ: I brought a woman.

(*The* BARON *looks astonished. Then yelps with laughter.*)

BARON: Oh, *what* a good idea! What a *stroke!* Where is
she?

(*He looks around.*)

KUNZ: That's the point. Later on, we'll all have to
guess.

BARON: And find out! Marvellous! We'll unmask her.
I'll offer a prize to the man who strips her.

KUNZ: And, I think, a punishment for anyone who is
mistaken.

BARON: Exactly. What fun! I do enjoy these things. I
wish we could have one every month. I'm so glad
you liked Ferdy.

KUNZ: How long is it now?

BARON: Three years.

KUNZ: Long time.

BARON: For me. Let's be honest, for nearly all of us.
And women. No, three years is a big bite out of a
lifetime when you never know when it may come to
an end, or what you may have missed. But he's
very kind. He's still young. But his growing old
gnaws at me a bit, you know. Not that he still
doesn't look pretty good in the raw. Oh, he does.
But about me, he doesn't mind at all.

KUNZ: Who's the little flower with Redl?

BARON: No idea. *Something's* made her wilt. They've both just come from the Hofball.

KUNZ: So have I.

BARON: Of course. Poor you. And with your lady escort. I wonder if I'll spot her.
(*He stares around.*)
That's her!

KUNZ: That is the doorman at the Klomser Hotel.

BARON: Oh! I see I'm not going to. What on earth made you go to the Hofball?

KUNZ: I thought it might be amusing to go there first.
(KUNZ *nods at* REDL, *who is being captivated by* FERDY, *and starting to get recurring fits of giggles.*)
Look at the Colonel.

BARON: (*pleased*). He's enjoying himself.

KUNZ: I've never seen him like that before.

BARON: How many people have seen *you?* He's letting his hair down. What's left of it. It's starting to go. I noticed just now. He's a handsome devil.

KUNZ: Very.

BARON: And a brilliant officer, they say. Suppose you should be if you're at the top in counter espionage.

KUNZ: Preferably. He works morning and night.

BARON: He's only a railway clerk's son, did you know? So I suppose he's had to. Work, I mean. But he plays too. Look at him.
(REDL *and* FERDY *are swopping stories and giggling intermittently and furiously.* REDL *tries to light another cigar, but he can scarcely get it going. The* TSARINA *watches blankly and happily.*)
He told me once how hard he'd tried to change.

KUNZ: Hey, you! Little Shepherdess!
(*He takes a drink from a blushing* SHEPHERDESS.)
Beautiful. Yes?

BARON: Tried everything, apparently. Resolutions, vows, religion, medical advice, self-exhaustion. Used

to flog a dozen horses into the ground in a day.
And then gardening, if you please, fencing and all
those studies they do, you do, of course—military
history, ciphers, telegraphy, campaigns, he knows,
hundreds of them, by heart. He knows his German
literature, speaks superb French and Russian,
Italian, Polish, Czech *and* Turkish if you please.

KUNZ: Not bad for a Ruthenian railway clerk.

BARON: As you say. Oh, take your eye off Redl. He's
not after the Tsarina. Or Ferdy. Is he? No, I don't
think so. He's just being himself for once. Don't
you think we should all form an Empire of our
own?

KUNZ: What's that?

BARON: Well, instead of all joining together, you know,
one Empire of sixty million Germans, like they're
always going on about. What about an Empire of
us. Ex million queens.

KUNZ: Who would there be?

BARON: Well, you and me for a start. I'd be Minister of
Culture, I think. REDL could catch any spies,
women spies. And you could do what you liked.

KUNZ: And who else?

BARON: Not Jews I think. They're the least queer in my
opinion. Their mothers won't let them. Germans,
Prussians, they're *very* queer. All that duelling.
Poles, not so much.

KUNZ: Italians?

BARON: No, they're like women, only better, women con
brio. Hungarians are just goats, of course, but
some are quite nice. French: too spry to let life play
a trick on *them*.

KUNZ: What about the English?

BARON: Next, after the Germans.

KUNZ: I agree with that. Queen Victoria was quite
clearly a man.

BARON: But *she* was a German, wasn't she?

KUNZ: Ah, yes. Still, you're right about the English.

BARON: I believe Redl has an Eton straw boater hanging over his bed as a trophy. They say it belongs to the younger son of the British Ambassador.
(*Pause.*)
How's that son of yours?
(KUNZ *looks immediately on guard.*)
I was only asking.

KUNZ: He's well.

BARON: I'm sorry. It must be difficult. If people *will* get married.

KUNZ: Well, *I* did.

BARON: The boy knows nothing?

KUNZ: Nothing.

BARON: His mother hasn't——

KUNZ: No. And she won't.

BARON: Why not? Doesn't she——

KUNZ: She pretends.

BARON: Ah! They *do*. And the boy?

KUNZ: *He's* all right, if that's what you mean.

BARON: You mean you're *not* all right?

KUNZ: Who knows? Is this Redl's flower?
(STEFAN *approaches.*)

BARON: Yes. My dear boy, you must meet the Major Advocate Kunz. Lieutenant—I'm sorry——?

STEFAN: Kovacs.
(*They salute.*)

BARON: Hungarian. Did you enjoy the terrace? I knew you would. Oh, thank heaven the music's stopped. Alfred's been having the giggles with little Ferdy while you've been away. Do have another glass, dear boy.
(REDL *and* FERDY *stand up, giggling helplessly. The others listen.*)

FERDY: And the manager, said, he said to me: we don't allow ladies in here, in here without male escorts.
(REDL *doubles up.*)

84

And, so I pointed at the Baron and said, what do you think *he* is!

(REDL *falls on the* TSARINA *who squeals*.)

KUNZ: (*to* STEFAN). Is this your first visit to this kind of thing?

STEFAN: Yes, sir.

BARON: Oh, don't call him sir. Just because he's dressed as Nelson. He's only an old Army lawyer. I must say you look very fine with that black patch. We must find a Lady Hamilton for him before the evening's out, mustn't we? I was saying, where do you keep your arm?

(KUNZ *leaves it out of his tunic, and stretches it*.)

Ah, there it is, you see?

KUNZ: That's better.

BARON: You danced very well, all the same.

KUNZ: (*to* STEFAN). Would you care to?

(STEFAN *is slightly confused for a moment*.)

STEFAN: Thank you, I'm a bit hot.

BARON: Must be cold on that terrace.

KUNZ: You see, this is a place for people to come together. People who are very often in their every-day lives, rather lonely and even miserable and feel hunted. As if they had a spy catcher like the Colonel on their heels.

STEFAN: Of course. I understand that.

KUNZ: And, because of the Baron's panache and generosity—and, let's be frank, recklessness——

BARON: Look's who's talking——

KUNZ: They come together and become something else. Like sinners in a church.

(FERDY *stands up*.)

LADY GODIVA: Two monks in the street.

TSARINA: I *like* monks.

LADY GODIVA: Two monks. Walking in the street. One's saying his rosary to himself. The other passes by as he's saying 'Hail Mary'. And the other stops and says: 'Hullo, Ursula.'

85

(REDL *collapses. So does* FERDY. *Then recovers
professionally. The others watch, and some of the
dancers too, including* KUPFER *and* ALBRECHT-
COLUMBINE, *and* FIGARO *and* LADY GODIVA.
General laughter. The BARON *is pleased.* FERDY *sits
back next to* REDL *and they both drink and giggle
together, mostly at nothing, until later in the scene when*
REDL *takes in* KUPFER *and becomes hostile: to*
KUPFER, *drunkenness and himself.*

KUNZ: You're not enjoying yourself much. (*Small pause.*)
Are you?

(STEFAN *blushes.*)

STEFAN: Not at all.

KUNZ: You mustn't judge the world at carnival time.
There is such a thing, such a contract, such a bond
as marriage——

BARON: You should know, poor soul.

KUNZ: And there is friendship, comradeship. In the
midst of all this, I ask you not to sneer, or I will
beat your sanctimonious head in——

BARON: Jaroslaw——

KUNZ: Aristotle, if you've heard of him.

STEFAN: I have——

BARON: Please; take no notice . . .

KUNZ: I'm glad to hear it. Says it can be either good, or
pleasant or useful. Which is true, but not always.
But he also says it lasts in such men only, only as
long as they keep their goodness. And goodness,
unfortunately, Lieutenant, does not last.

STEFAN: No?

KUNZ: No. And don't be insolent.

STEFAN: Then don't be offensive.

BARON: Tempers, darlings, tempers!

KUNZ: It seldom lasts shall we say? But then such men
are rare, anyway.

(*The other guests gather round, and listen, and begin to take
part. During this sequence,* REDL *sobers up and stiffens.*)

86

KUPFER: Good evening, Colonel Redl.

REDL: I don't . . .

KUPFER: *Now* you do . . .

BARON: *Everyone!* Met *everyone* before. (*To* ALBRECHT.)

KUPFER: Kupfer. Major Kupfer, sir. General Staff. Ninth Corps. Prague.

REDL: Prague, Prague . . . This is Vienna. What are you doing here?

KUPFER: Same as you, sir. On leave.

REDL: *I'm* not on leave.

KUPFER: I didn't necessarily mean literally——

REDL: You'll remember Steinbauer then?

KUPFER: Of course.

(*He greets the wimpled* STEINBAUER *casually.*)

It was a blow about Siczynski. (*Pause.*) Wasn't it?

REDL: Was it?

KUPFER: Wasn't he a particular friend of yours?

REDL: I scarcely knew him. We neither of us did . . .

KUPFER: Why did you agree to be his second? It wasn't a very correct thing for such a correct officer as you to be doing.

REDL: I thought he should have support . . . No one liked him.

KUPFER: But *you've* always been popular, Colonel.

REDL: Are you being . . . because if so . . .

KUPFER: You only have my admiration, Colonel. With all the advantages I was born with, I only wish I— could—ever go—so far. You seemed to be having an entertaining time just there, Colonel. Please don't let me——

FERDY: Don't you think he's beautiful? I adore it when he screws his monocle in his eye.

(REDL *doesn't think this at all funny, though the* BARON *and* KUNZ *are pleased, and, of course,* KUPFER. REDL *stands more erect than ever, and lights up a fresh cigar, grabbing a glass from the passing* SHEPHERDESS.)

REDL: Hey, you! Fräulein!

87

FERDY: Have you heard about that extraordinary Dr. Schoepfer?

KUPFER: No. Who is he?

FERDY: Don't you know? My dear, he sounds divine! The Tsarina went there last night.

STEINBAUER: What does he do?

FERDY: Just talks, my dear, for *hours*. Not a smile. Medical do's and all that, but, if you say you're a student, you can get in.

KUPFER: What's he talk about?

FERDY: Why, *us*. He sounds an absolute scream. Can't stop talking about it.

REDL: Us? Speak for yourself.

BARON: What's he say then, Ferdy?

FERDY: Oh, that we're all demented something, something cox on the end, darling.
(*Laughter.*)

LADY GODIVA: Well, he's right, of course.

FERDY: That we're all potential criminals, and some of us should even be castrated.
(*Screams.*)
And that we're a warning symptom of the crisis in, oh, civilization, and the decline in Christian whatnots.

BARON: Oh, and he goes on about marriage and the family being the basis of the Empire, and *we* must be rooted out. *She* says he's a scream.
(*They look at the* TSARINA, *who nods, giggles and goes crimson.*)

MARIE ANTOINETTE: Is he a Jew?

FERDY: But, of course, darling! She says he looks like Shylock's mother.

KUPFER: But who is he?

KUNZ: A neurologist, I believe. Nerves.

BARON: Well, I'm sure he'd get on mine.

KUNZ: I think he's one of those people who insist they can penetrate the inner secrets of your own nature.

BARON: I understand the inner secrets of my nature perfectly well. I don't admire them, but I do know them, anyway better than this Dr. Schoepfer.

FERDY: Silly mare!

BARON: And I'm quite happy as I am, I'm no criminal, thank you, and I don't corrupt anything that isn't already quite clearly corrupt, like this ghastly city. On the contrary, I bring style, wit, pleasure, energy and good humour to it that it wouldn't otherwise have.

KUPFER: Well said, Baron.

BARON: More drinks, everyone! And music! (*To* MUSICIANS.)

ALBRECHT: I went to a doctor once, and he just said 'pull your socks up'. Do you know what he told me to do? Go into the Army! (*Shrieks.*) And find yourself a nice girl. Get married. So: naturally, I went into the Army. Artillery. In the second week I'd been seduced by the Corporal of Horse *and* a sub-lieutenant.

BARON: Oh, I went to a doctor like a silly thing when I was a student. He just looked very agitated and told me there was nothing he could do and to go away. A few years later I heard he'd cut his throat . . .

MARIE ANTOINETTE: I plucked up courage to tell *our* family doctor, and I said I'd like to be sent away to some special clinic in Vienna . . . Well, I thought he was going to go raving mad. Vienna, he said, Vienna, *you* want to go to Vienna. I'll send you to hell. You'll find all you want *there*, you quivering, scheming little sissy!

ALBRECHT: When I first came to Vienna, it seemed like paradise, but now I do get a bit bored. Not here, of course, Baron. But you know what I mean. Same tired old exhibits. Nothing new ever seems to come in.

89

TSARINA: (*now sitting on the* BARON's *knee shyly*). I remember the first time a man tickled the palm of my hand with his middle finger, when we shook hands, and then later he told me what he was. I was very religious then, and I thought he was wicked. I really did at the time.

KUNZ: Perhaps you were right.

LADY GODIVA: *I* went to our priest. He quoted Aquinas and said anything that was against nature was against God . . . He always kept an eye on me afterwards, always pulling me up and asking me questions.

STEINBAUER: *My* priest said: you *can't* be like that. You're a soldier, a man of courage and honour and virtue. Your uniform itself embodies the glory of the Empire and the Church. I worshipped Radetzky at the time, and he knew it. So he said do you think someone like Radetzky could have ever been like that? I didn't know about Julius Caesar and Alexander then.

FIGARO: (*to* REDL, *who is like a frozen ox*). I hate these screamers, don't you?

LADY GODIVA: I used to go to the priest after I'd confessed I was in love with Fritz. Then I used to lie like crazy about it, and say nothing was happening, although we were having sex regularly. And he'd give me absolution and say, 'It may not take on immediately——'.
(*Laughter.*)

LADY GODIVA: If Fritz just moved his little finger at me, I'd go back. Then he went with a girl suddenly and got married. When she was pregnant, we had beers together, and he pinched my arm and kissed me. Then he laughed and said: You know what you are, find someone else the same. . . . But he laughed . . .

FERDY: I should think so, you soppy little thing.
(FERDY *is bored with all this and wants attention.*)
I only went to a doctor once and he just said take
more exercise, dear. So I did.
(*He executes a skilful entrechat to general amusement till*
REDL *strikes him hard across the face, knocking him down
right into the other guests. The boy is stunned by the force
of it. Silence.*)
REDL: Baron—forgive me.
(*He clicks his heels and goes, followed presently by*
STEFAN *in silence. Then the* BARON *booms out over a
few 'Wells!', etc.*
BARON: Someone pick up poor Ferdy. You silly boy! I
knew you shouldn't have flirted with Colonel Redl.
He's a dangerous man. Are you better? There now!
Come along, everybody, that's quite enough
melodrama. On with the ball—I suppose——
(*They reassemble. Lights lower. And they hear the
spirit of Mozart as* FERDY *sings, not without some
sweetness, 'Vedrai Carino' or 'Batti, Batti'. Or something
similar which is tolerably within his range.*)

FADE

91

Scene 2

Lecture Room. Rostrum. A glass of water. DR. SCHOEPFER *is speaking.*

SCHOEPFER: The *evasion*, naturally, of responsibility . . .
For instance in enjoying the physical sensations of
the body without any reference to the responsi-
bilities involved in the relationship. Or, indeed, to
society or any beliefs, such as a belief in God. They
can never, in their ignorance, some men say folly,
in their infirmity, never attain that complete love,
the love that only is possible between men and
women, whose shared interests . . .
(*There is a suppressed giggle.*)
. . . whose shared interests include the blessed gift
of children and grandchildren which alone, I
think, most people would agree even today, which
alone gives a grand and enduring purpose to
sexual congress.
(*He drinks from the glass of water.*)
Now, gentlemen: these traits are caused by
regression to the phallic stage of libido develop-
ment, and can be traced to what is in fact a flight
from incest . . .

FADE

Scene 3

A hill clearing outside Dresden, surrounded by fir trees. Cold winter. OBLENSKY *is warmly wrapped up in his greatcoat, sitting on a tree trunk smoking a cigarette.* STANITSIN *stands beside him.*

STANITSIN: Here he comes.

OBLENSKY: To the minute. As you'd expect. You'd better give me the file. Oh, just a minute, have you got the parcel I asked for?

(STANITSIN *nods.*)

It wasn't easy this week getting in. The boy Kovacs is staying there while he's commanding this exercise.

(REDL *enters, smoking a cigar. He looks cool and sure of himself.*)

REDL: Mr. Smith?

OBLENSKY: Yes, indeed. Rather *this* is Mr. Smith.

REDL: Look, I haven't time to waste fooling about——

OBLENSKY: Quite. You got our message, and, blessedly, you are here, Colonel Redl.

REDL: And who the devil are you?

OBLENSKY: Colonel Oblensky.

REDL: Oblensky . . .

(OBLENSKY *waits for the effect to take, and goes on.*)

OBLENSKY: It won't take you long, Colonel. I know your regiment is waiting for you . . . loosely speaking. I have a file here, which I would like to acquaint you with briefly. Would you care to sit down?

(REDL *doesn't move.*)

Just a matter of minutes. I have no anxiety about you reaching for your revolver to shoot either of us. I know you will realise that all this file is duplicated both in Warsaw *and* St. Petersburg. What I do beg of you is to pause before you think of turning it on yourself. I think we can find a satisfactory, and probably long-term arrangement which will work out quite well for all of us, and no trouble.

REDL: (*recovering, coldly*). May I see?

OBLENSKY: Naturally, oh, this is Lieutenant Stanitsin.
(STANITSIN *bows*.)

REDL: Mr. Smith?

STANITSIN: My pen name, sir.
(REDL *puts out his hand impatiently for the file.*
OBLENSKY *hands him the contents in batches. They watch*
REDL *flip through, stone faced.*)

REDL: Mess bills in Lemberg! Eighteen eighty-nine! Tailors' bills, jeweller's, stables, coachbuilders, tobacconists. What *is* all this? They're just bills.

OBLENSKY: Rather unusual bills for a young officer of no independent means.

REDL: I have an uncle——

OBLENSKY: You have no uncle, Colonel. Two brothers only. Both happily married—and penniless.
(*Hands him another bill.*)
Cartiers. One gold cigarette case inscribed 'to dearest Stefan with love, Alfred'.

REDL: My nephew.
(OBLENSKY *hasn't the heart to smile at this.* REDL's *immediate humiliation is so evident.*)

OBLENSKY: Your bank statements from the Austro-Hungarian Bank in both Vienna and Prague for the month of February.
(REDL *hardly looks at them. Pause.*)

REDL: Well?

OBLENSKY: I'm sorry, Colonel. We'll soon get this over. One letter, date, February 17th 1901. 'My darling,

94

don't be angry. When I make no sign, you know or
should know, that I love you. Please see me again.
All I long for is to lie beside you, nothing else. I
don't know what to do to kill the time before I see
you again, and watch you, how I can do something
to pass the time.'

REDL: It is no crime to write a love letter, Colonel, even
if it isn't in the style of Pushkin.

OBLENSKY: The style's tolerable enough for a man in
love. . . . But this letter is not addressed to a woman.

REDL: There's no name on it.

OBLENSKY: There is on the envelope.

REDL: *Not* very convincing, Colonel.

OBLENSKY: Very well. Those—if you'd just glance
through them quickly—are signed affidavits
from——

(REDL *won't look at them. He has mustered himself
wonderfully. He feels the chance of a small hope.*)

(*politely, casually*). The page at the Grand Hotel, a
musician at the Volksgarten—this is only the last
six weeks, you understand—a waiter at Sacher's, a
Corporal in the Seventh Corps in Prague, a
boatman in Vienna, a pastry cook, a compositor on
the 'Deutsches Volksblatt' and a *reporter* on the
'Neue Freie Presse'. (*Pause.*) One right-wing paper,
one liberal, eh?

(REDL *puffs on his cigar.*)

REDL: (*slowly*). Whores. Bribed, perjuring whores.

OBLENSKY: Yes. Against the word of a distinguished
officer in the Royal Imperial Army. . . . Oh, dear
. . . Stanitsin. Photographs. . . .

(STANITSIN *hands a bundle of large photographs to* REDL
*who looks at the first four or five. Then he hands them back.
Pause. He sits on another trunk and slowly puts his face in
his hands.*)

Offer the Colonel some brandy.

(STANITSIN *offers him a flask, which he drinks from.*)

95

I think *I'll* have some, Stanitsin. Now that's all over,
let us all have some. Forgive me, Colonel. Now:
time is short for us. What you decide to do is up
to you. There are three courses open to you. One
we have mentioned. The second is to leave the
Army. The third is to remain in the Army and
continue with your brilliant career. Do you know
what Russia spent on espionage last year. Colonel?
Nine million roubles. Nine. This year it will be
even more. What do your people spend? Half? No,
I've watched you for more than ten years, and
you'd be surprised probably, or perhaps I'm wrong,
about how much I know about the kind of man you
are. What can you do? Change your way of life?
It's getting desperate already, isn't it? You don't
know which way to turn, you're up to your eye-
balls in debts. What could you do? Get thrown out,
exposed for everything you are, or what the world
would say you are. Would you, do you think,
could you change your way of life, what else do you
want after all these years, what would you do at
your age, go back to base and become a waiter or
a washer up, sit all alone in cafés again constantly
watching? What are you fit for?
(*His tone relaxes.*)
The same as me, my dear friend, the same as me,
and very good indeed you are at it, soldiering, war
and treachery, or the treachery that leads to wars.
The game. It's a fine one. And no one's better at it
in Europe than me—at the moment. (*Smiles.*) Heavy
turnover sometimes. Tell me, do none of your
brother officers know or suspect?

REDL: Kovacs, Kupfer, Steinbauer . . . No.

OBLENSKY: And Kunz? Kunz's only real indiscretion is
the Baron's annual ball, and he could always say
he went as a relation or even as a tourist even
though it's hardly respectable. We've never caught

him out in all these years, have we, Stanitsin? He
does . . . doesn't he . . .?

REDL: I assume so.

OBLENSKY: The other two, Steinbauer and Kupfer,
well, they seem to have left wormcasts all over
Europe, so they're no threat to you. And Kovacs,
he's only—been—with *you*, hasn't he?

REDL: Yes.

OBLENSKY: Sure?

REDL: (*wryly*). Colonel Oblensky, I may find myself
here before you, in this position, but I remind you
that I *am* an officer in the Austrian Chief of Staff's
Counter Espionage Department. *I* know how to
interrogate myself. The answer's yes.
(OBLENSKY *smiles*.)

OBLENSKY: Oh, I'm the last to under-estimate you,
Colonel. Last report from General Staff Head-
quarters January 5th: 'supremely capable, learned,
intuitive and precise in command, tactful, excellent
manners.' And now your handling of the corps
exercise on Monday: 'He is uncommonly striking.
Both as a battalion and regimental commander.'
And there's your Regiment, the 77th Infantry.
Didn't the Emperor call it 'my beautiful Seventy
Seventh'. Oh, you certainly chose the right career,
Colonel. Cigarette? I think the really interesting
thing about you, Redl, is that you yourself are
really properly aware of your own distinction—as
you should be. If you ever do feel any shame for
what you are, you don't accept it like a simpleton,
you heave it off, like a horse that's fallen on you.
And the result is, I suppose what they mean by that
splendid Viennese style. Ah, the time, yes, we must
be going. Give the Colonel his package.
(STANITSIN *does so*.)

REDL: Is that all?

OBLENSKY: You must be returning to the regiment, Colonel.

REDL: What's this?

OBLENSKY: Mr. Smith will contact you when you've
had a few days to rest and recover generally. The
package contains seven thousand kronen in notes.
. . . Far more than *you* pay, Colonel.
(REDL *puts it in his pocket slowly, collects himself, and
bows.*)
Goodbye, Colonel. I don't suppose we shall meet
again for a long time—if ever . . . It *is* a little
risky, even for you, isn't it?
(*He laughs, full of good humour.*)
Oh, Stanitsin, the parcel.
(*He hands a paper bag to* REDL, *who, puzzled, takes
from it an Etonian straw boater.*)
Perhaps you should return it to the British
Ambassador.
(*He laughs heartily.*)
Forgive me, Colonel, but I do have a very clumsy,
clumsy sense of humour sometimes. No, always!
(STANITSIN *smiles and goes out. The two men watch him.
Presently they hear his laughter floating back through the
woods.*)

CURTAIN

END OF ACT II

ACT III *Scene 1*

REDL's *apartment in Vienna. Baroque, luxurious. It is late afternoon, the curtains are drawn, the light comes through them and two figures can just be seen in bed. One is* REDL *who appears to be asleep. The other, the figure of a* YOUNG MAN, *is getting up very quietly, almost stealthily, and dressing. There is a rattle of coins and jewellery.*

REDL: Don't take my cigarette case, will you? *Or* my watch.
(*The boy hesitates.*)
There's plenty of change. Take that. Go on. Now you'd better . . . hurry back.
(*The boy slips out quickly, expertly.* REDL *sits up and lights a cigar. He gets up and puts on a beautiful dressing gown. Presently* KUPFER *comes in.*)
Who's that? Oh, you? Why don't you knock?
KUPFER: I knew you were alone.
REDL: What's the time?
KUPFER: Four. Shall I open the shutters?
(*He does so.* REDL *shrinks a little.*)
REDL: That's enough.
KUPFER: The sun's quite hot.
(*He sits in an armchair by the window.*)
I waited. Till your little friend left.
REDL: Very courteous. Well?
KUPFER: I've news.
REDL: Bad, no doubt.
KUPFER: Afraid so.
REDL: Out with it.

99

KUPFER: Stefan was married secretly this morning.
(*Pause.*) To the Countess Delyanoff.
(*Pause.*)

REDL: Naturally. The bitch . . . Does she want to see
me?

KUPFER: Why, yes—she's waiting.

REDL: Well, go and get her. And then go away.
(KUPFER *turns.*)
No. Wait outside.
(KUPFER *goes and* REDL *smokes his cigar, looking out
of the window. Soon the* COUNTESS *enters.*)

COUNTESS: Alfred?

REDL: So: you pulled it off.

COUNTESS: Alfred. We've endured all of that. Can't
we——

REDL: No. What's he doing, marrying *you?*

COUNTESS: He loves me. No more . . .

REDL: I suppose you're calving.

COUNTESS: I'm having his child, Alfred.

REDL: I knew it! Knew it!

COUNTESS: He *would* have married me. He was disgusted
by your behaviour.

REDL: Oh?

COUNTESS: You must admit, Alfred, telling him I was
Jewish wasn't very subtle—for *you.*

REDL: Well, you are, aren't you? And I don't believe
you'd told him.

COUNTESS: No, I hadn't. But my *not* telling him was
cowardly, not vulgar, like yours *was.* You surprise
me, Alfred.

REDL: And he'll have to resign his commission as he's
no means?

COUNTESS: He wants to go into journalism.

REDL: And become a politician.

COUNTESS: Alfred, we had such feeling for each other
once.

REDL: I didn't, you Jewish prig, you whited sepulchre,

does he know what you really are, apart from a
whore, a whoring spy?

COUNTESS: No. He doesn't. No one knows. Except you.
It's extraordinary you should have kept it a secret,
but I don't expect you to behave differently now.

REDL: Don't count on it. . . . You little Jewish spy——

COUNTESS: I'm not, not now, Alfred, you know . . . it
was my husband, when he was alive——

REDL: Don't snivel. You took *me* in.

COUNTESS: I didn't. I loved you . . .

REDL: Well, I didn't love you. I love Stefan. *We* just
fooled one another. Oh, I tried to hoax myself too,
but not really often. So: tonight's your wedding
night. (*Pause.*) I tell you this: you'll never know
that body like I know it. The lines beneath his eyes.
Do you know how many there are, do you know
one has less than the other? And the scar behind
his ear, and the hairs in his nostrils, which has the
most, what colour they are in what light? The mole
on where? Where, Sophia? I know the place here,
between the eyes, the dark patches like slate—like
blue when he's tired, really tired, the place for a
blow or a kiss or a bullet. You'll never know like I
know, you can't. The backs of his knees, the pattern
on the soles of his feet. Which trouble him, and so
I used to wash them and bathe them for hours.
His thick waist, and how long are his thighs,
compared to his calves, you've not looked at him,
you never will.

COUNTESS: Stop it!

(*Pause.*)

REDL: You don't know what to do with that. And now
you've got it.

COUNTESS: God, I'm weary of your self-righteousness and
all your superior railing and your glib cant about
friendship and the Army and the way you all roll
out your little parade: Michelangelo and Socrates,

and Alexander and Leonardo. God, you're like a
guild of housewives pointing out Catherine the
Great.

REDL: So: you'll turn Stefan into another portly
middle-aged father with—what did you say once—
snotty little longings under their watch chains and
glances at big, unruptured bottoms.

COUNTESS: Alfred: every one of *you* ends up, as you well
know, with a bottom quite different, much
plumper and far wider than any ordinary man.

REDL: You think, people like you, you've got a formula
for me. You think I'm hobbled, as you say. But I'm
free of you, anyway. You, what about you, I can
resist you!

COUNTESS: Do you know, remember, what you once
said to me: I can never blame you. You are my
heart.

REDL: I do blame you. I was lying. And Stefan is my heart.
(*Pause.*)

COUNTESS: He said you told him I was Jewish. And
what I looked like, what I *would* look like, drooping
hairy skin and flab, and so on——

REDL: And now you're going to be a mother. You
think you're a river or something, I suppose.

COUNTESS: That's right, Alfred. A sewer. Your old
temple built over a sewer.

REDL: Sophia, why don't we . . .?

COUNTESS: No, Alfred. I'm in your grip. But I'll make
no bargains. Do as you wish.

REDL: I bought him a beautiful new gelding last week.

COUNTESS: It should be back in your stables by now.
And your groom's got all the other——

REDL: Get out.

COUNTESS: I'm going, Alfred. Do as you wish. You may
think a trick was played on you once, but you've
repaid and re-played it a thousand times over. I
pity you: really——

REDL: Don't then. I'm really doing quite well.

(*She goes out.* KUPFER *comes in.*)

KUPFER: Well?

REDL: Well? Nothing. . . . I suppose you think you're moving in?

KUPFER: Do you want me to draw up a full report on your file on the Countess?

REDL: That file is *my* property. And *you'll* do as you're told. I'm going to sleep. Close the shutters.

(KUPFER *does so.* REDL *falls asleep almost immediately on the bed. Soon little moaning noises are heard from him.* KUPFER *smokes a cigarette in the early evening light.*)

FADE

Scene 2

The Red Lounge of the Sacher Hotel, Vienna. A string orchestra plays. REDL *and* KUPFER *are drinking together.* KUPFER *is in a sour, watching mood.* REDL *is even cooler than usual and is smoking and appraising the other occupants of the lounge. He hails a* WAITER.

REDL: (*to* KUPFER). Another?

KUPFER: No. I'm going.

REDL: (*to the* WAITER). Just one then. So soon?
  (*Pause.*)

KUPFER: Why St. Petersburg, for heaven's sake?

REDL: Because I've signed the order, and General Staff is not equipped to countermand orders. It works on the sweet Viennese roundabout method. Anyway, there's no one else.

KUPFER: But a whole year. I don't even speak Russian. It's nonsense.

REDL: Not to the Bureau. And now you *can* learn Russian, as I did. You should pick it up in half that time. It's the vowels that'll bring *you* down.

KUPFER: Thank you.

REDL: I'll get you back before the year's out. Don't worry.

KUPFER: You *are* sure of yourself, aren't you?

REDL: I have to be, don't I? And why not?
  (*He takes his drink from* WAITER.)
  No one is interested in doubts. This is an age of iron certainties, that's what they want to know about, run by money makers, large armies, munitions men, money makers for money makers. *You* were born

104

with a silver sabre up your whatnot.
(*Lifts his glass.*)
St. Petersburg! I'll give you some names and
addresses.

KUPFER: If only you'd at least admit it's because of
Mischa. Why can't you be honest?

REDL: Because honesty is no use to you. People who
don't want it are always yelling the place down for
it like some grizzling kid. When they get it they're
always miserable. . . . Besides, Mischa is getting
married, as you know.

KUPFER: I thought you'd put the stopper on that.

REDL: I didn't think we should tie him to a girl in a
confectionery shop, a broad-faced, big-hipped little
housefrau who can hardly read and write, and,
what's more, doesn't care, all chocolates and child-
birth. Still, if he wants that, he shall have it. It's a
poor reward. Sad, too . . .

KUPFER: You do pick them, don't you?

REDL: Yes . . . But that is the nature of it. Marriage has
never occurred to *you* for instance, has it?
(*Pause.*)
Since Stefan I've let them go their own ways. If
that's all, if that's the sum of it, if that's what they
want. . . .

KUPFER: At least be honest with your*self*. The girl came
round again last night.

REDL: Did she then? I told Max to throw her out. Next
time he'll throw her down the stairs.

KUPFER: Then *she'll* end up in hospital as well.

REDL: Damn it, he's only got a nervous breakdown, or
whatever they call it nowadays.

KUPFER: She says he's off his head.

REDL: Nonsense. He's always been over-strung. Maybe
a bit unbalanced. He'll recover. And then he can
marry her.

KUPFER: And he calls *me* cruel!

105

REDL: *You* were born like it. All your sort of people are. It's expected of you.

KUPFER: And what about *your* sort of people then?

REDL: Sometimes it's inescapable. I'm still nicer than you, Kupfer.

KUPFER: Why do you hate me, Alfred?
(*Pause.*)
Why then?

REDL: I've said often enough no one, and not you, is to call me Alfred in public . . . (*Hesitates.*)

KUPFER: Then why do you let me live with you?

REDL: You don't. I allow you a room in my apartment.

KUPFER: Exactly. You know, better than anyone, about jealousy.

REDL: It's a discipline, like Russian. You master it, or you don't. It's up to you, isn't it? Ah, here's Hötzendorf and Möhl.

KUPFER: Who's the boy?

REDL: Try and restrain your curiosity a little.
(*They rise and greet* GENERAL HÖTZENDORF, GENERAL MÖHL *and* SUB-LIEUTENANT VIKTOR JERZABEK. *All salute stiffly, aware of their own presence in the lounge.*)

HÖTZENDORF: Ah, Colonel, the Lieutenant tells me that great automobile and chauffeur outside belong to you.

REDL: Yes, sir. New toy, I'm afraid.

HÖTZENDORF: Expensive toy. Don't see many like that. Thought it must belong to some fat Jew.
(REDL *is discomfited.*)
Oh, don't misunderstand me, the vehicle itself is in impeccable taste, Redl, like everything to do with you.

REDL: Will you join us, sir?

HÖTZENDORF: Just having a quick dinner. Brought some work with us, then back to the office.

MÖHL: The Lieutenant is the only one who seems able to take down the General's notes fast enough.

HÖTZENDORF: Well, quickly then. I wanted a word
with you.

REDL: Waiter! I was just celebrating some good fortune.
My uncle in Galicia has just left me a legacy.
(*Chairs are feverishly placed round the table for the
arrivals. Everyone sits and orders.*)

HÖTZENDORF: Well done. Good. Yes, very good taste.
Though I still prefer a good pair of horses, can't
run an army with automobiles. No, but you know
it's not that the Jews themselves are specially rotten.
It's what they represent. For instance, no belief in
service, and how can the Empire survive without
the idea of service? Look at the Jews in Galicia,
you must know, Redl, getting them into the army
—quite impossible.

REDL: Indeed. *And* the high percentage of desertion.

MÖHL: Really? I didn't know that.

REDL: Nineteen per cent.

HÖTZENDORF: There you are. They're outsiders, they
feel outsiders, so their whole creed of life must be
based on duplicity—by necessity.

REDL: I agree, sir. Even their religion seems to be little
more than a series of rather pious fads.

HÖTZENDORF: Quite. We're all Germans, all of us, and
that's the way of it. At least: Jews when they get
on, remind us of it.

REDL: Which I suppose is a useful function.

HÖTZENDORF: Talking of that, Redl, I want to congratulate you on your handling of that Cracow spy
affair. Everyone, absolutely everyone's most
impressed and highly delighted, including the
Emperor himself.

REDL: I'm deeply honoured, sir.

HÖTZENDORF: Well. You do honour to us. I see you
already have the order of the Iron Crown Second
Class. Möhl here is recommending you for the
Military Service Medal.

REDL: I don't know what——

HÖTZENDORF: You know your stuff, Redl. You've an extraordinary understanding and intuition as far as the criminal intelligence is concerned. And, there it is, spies are criminals like any other. We all just use them like any thief or murderer.

MÖHL: That's right, he's right.

HÖTZENDORF: Cracow is our first bastion against Russia. If war breaks out, it's imperative those fortresses don't crack. They'll go for them first. If that little ring you rounded up had succeeded, we could have lost a war the day it started. From April I am proposing that you take over the Prague Bureau. Rumpler will direct Vienna.

REDL: I'm overwhelmed, sir.

MÖHL: To be confirmed of course.

REDL: Of course.

(HOTZENDORF *raises his glass.*)

HÖTZENDORF: Congratulations, Colonel. To your continued success in Prague.

(*They drink the toast. The three arrivals rise at a signal.*) Well, gentlemen. Goodbye, Redl. Oh, this young man tells me he's your nephew.

REDL: That's right, sir.

HÖTZENDORF: Good. Well, the General Staff can do with all the Redls there are around.

(*Salute. They pass through the lounge.* REDL *sits.* KUPFER *is dumbfounded.*)

REDL: Rumpler *would* stay in Vienna, naturally, with his coat of arms. Still, Prague . . .

KUPFER: Nephew!

REDL: Not yet. But I can't let an unknown Lieutenant from nowhere ride about Vienna in my new Austro-Daimler Phaeton. And I promised him faithfully the other day he could drive it himself sometime. He's quite clever mechanically.

(KUPFER *turns on his heel, and goes out.* REDL *lights*

a cigar and nods to the HEAD WAITER.)

Send me the waiter over. I want the bill.

WAITER: Yes, sir.

REDL: No, not him. The young one.

FADE

Scene 3

Hospital Ward. High, bare and chill. In an iron bed, sitting up, is a young man, MISCHA LIPSCHUTZ. *Beside him is a young girl,* MITZI HEIGEL. *The sound of boots striking smartly on the cold floor of a hospital corridor.* REDL *enters briskly. In greatcoat, gloves, carrying cane. An* ORDERLY *comes up to him respectfully.*

ORDERLY: Colonel, sir.

REDL: Colonel von Redl. To see Mischa Lipschutz.

ORDERLY: At once, Colonel, sir.

> (*He leads him to* MISCHA's *bed.* MISCHA *hardly takes him in.* MITZI *looks up, then down again, as if she has become numbed by sitting in the same cold position so long.*)

ORDERLY: Shall I tell the young lady to go?

REDL: No. Mischa. How are you? I've brought you a hamper.

> (*No response. He hands it to the* ORDERLY.)
> See that he gets all of it. Are you feeling any better? When do you think you'll be out then, eh? You look quite well, you know. . . . Perhaps you're still not rested enough. . . . Mischa . . . (*To* ORDERLY.) Can't he hear me? He looks all right.

ORDERLY: Perhaps your voice sounds strange, just a fraction, sir? Mischa: Colonel Redl is here.

MISCHA: Mischa.

ORDERLY: How are you, the Colonel's asking?

MISCHA: I've been here quite a long time. I don't quite know how long, because we're absorbed into the air at night, and then, of course they can do anything they like with you at will. But that's why I keep rather quiet.

REDL: Who, Mischa?

MISCHA: They do it with rays, I believe, and atoms and
they can send them from anywhere, right across
the world, and fill you up with them and germs and
all sorts of things.

REDL: Mischa, do you know where you are?

MISCHA: On a star, sir, on a star. Just like you. I expect
you were sent to Vienna too, sir, because you are
the same kind of element as me. The same dual
body functioning.

(REDL *stands back. The* ORDERLY *shrugs, the* GIRL
doesn't look up. REDL *walks out quickly.*)

FADE

Scene 4

An hotel room near the Polish border in Galicia. It is cheap, filled with smoke but quite cosy. OBLENSKY *is sprawled on a low sofa, his tunic open, relaxed, hot with much vodka.* REDL *is slightly drunk too, though less cheerful.*

OBLENSKY: Come here, over here, have some more. Where are you, Redl, you're always disappearing? Why are you so restless always? All the time limping home with scars, and now you've got a bitten lip, I see. Tell me now, about this new boy, what's it—Viktor——

REDL: He's not new.

OBLENSKY: I thought it was last February.

REDL: December.

OBLENSKY: Five months! Oh, I suppose that is a long time for you.

REDL: How often are you unfaithful to your wife?

OBLENSKY: When I'm not working too hard, and if I can arrange it, daily.

REDL: You seem to arrange most things.

OBLENSKY: Don't say it in that tone of voice. I was looking it up the other day. You've had eighty thousand kronen out of me over the years.

REDL: Out of Mother Russia.

OBLENSKY: Quite so. And she can ill afford your way of life.

REDL: She's had her money's worth.

OBLENSKY: Not over Cracow.

REDL: Oh, not again.

OBLENSKY: Well, later. Tell me about what's it, Viktor?
   Is he handsome?
REDL: Extremely.
OBLENSKY: Yes, but how handsome, in what way?
REDL: Tall, fair, eyes pale . . .
OBLENSKY: Is that what you like? Watery?
REDL: Tell me what *you* like.
OBLENSKY: My dear friend, ha!
   (*He roars with laughter.*)
   Nothing has the enduring, unremitting crudity of
   what I like. And *no* interest. I like nothing exotic.
   Now, the Countess, you know, Delyanoff, you used
   to write those strained love letters to, I could have
   had her at any time, naturally. But, nothing, no
   interest, here, whatsoever.
   (*He crosses himself.*)
   Too exotic. And I suppose intelligent. I can under-
   stand *you* trying her out very well. All I want is a
   lump, a rump, a big, jolly roaring and boring, let
   us have no illusion, heaving lovely, wet and
   friendly, large and breasty lump!
   (*He roars, jumps up laughing, and fills their glasses.*)
   What I wouldn't do for one now! Yes, with you
   here too, Redl! Would that disgust you?
REDL: No.
OBLENSKY: Flicker of interest?
REDL: Very little. I *have* watched.
OBLENSKY: Oh, dear. You make me feel cruder than
   ever. Tears of Christ! I'd make her jump and giggle
   and give her fun. All girls like fun. Even if they're
   educated. Do you give fun? Much?
REDL: Some, I imagine. Perhaps not too much. If I
   liked anyone it was because they were beautiful,
   to me, anyway.
OBLENSKY: Yes, I see. That's quite different. I don't
   see very much beauty. I mean I don't need it.
   You're a romantic. You lust after the indescribable,

113

describe it, to yourself at least, and it becomes unspeakable.

REDL: You sound like a drunken Russian Oscar Wilde.

OBLENSKY: Me? Oscar Wilde!

(*He splutters with pleasure, and pours them out more vodka.*)

Perhaps there's a cosy chambermaid here, if they have such a thing in this hole. I'll ask Stanitsin. Do you get afraid very often?

REDL: Yes.

OBLENSKY: (*switching*). I'll tell you some things that stick in my throat about you people. Do you mind?

REDL: If you wish.

OBLENSKY: Well, one: you all assume you're the only ones who can understand anything about yourselves.

REDL: (*politely*). Yes?

OBLENSKY: Well, two: frankly you go on about beauty and lyricize away about naked bodies as if we were all gods.

REDL: Some of us.

OBLENSKY: Or else you carry on like—rutting pigs.

(*They both address each other in a friendly way across the barrier they both recognise immediately.*)

It isn't any fun having no clear idea of the future, is it? And you can't re-make your past. And then when one of you writes a book about yourselves, you pretend it's something else, that it's about married people and not two men together. . . . That is not honest, Alfred.

REDL: Don't be maudlin, Colonel.

OBLENSKY: Redl; you are one of those depressing people whom you always know you are bound to disappoint. And yet one tries. (*He looks quite jolly all the same.*) Well, you must be used to dancing at two weddings by this time. You've been doing it long enough.

REDL: You do enjoy despising me, don't you? Can we finish now?

OBLENSKY: Not till Cracow is settled. I don't despise you at all. Why should I? I don't care. I'm only curious.

REDL: My confessions are almost as entertaining as the Cracow fortifications.

OBLENSKY: You're quite wrong, quite, quite . . . I listen to you, I enjoy your company, see how much vodka we've drunk together, I don't drink with many people, Alfred. May I? I don't know anyone quite like you. It's taken a long time, hasn't it? You're giving nothing away this time.

REDL: What about Cracow?

OBLENSKY: Well, my dear friend, it was most embarrassing. Suddenly, my whole organisation pounced on —*poum!* And who did it! You!

REDL: It was unavoidable. I felt there were suspicions...

OBLENSKY: But no warnings . . .

REDL: I tried, but it had to be.

OBLENSKY: Hauser was about my best agent.

REDL: I'm sorry. But you might have lost *me* otherwise.

OBLENSKY: Maybe. But if *I* don't turn up with something, something *now*, I'll be roasted. You've got to *give* me someone. And someone significant I can parade at a big trial, like your affair. Well? (*Pause.*)

REDL: Very well. I have someone.

OBLENSKY: Who?

REDL: Kupfer.

OBLENSKY: Isn't he on your staff? St. Petersburg?

REDL: Yes.

OBLENSKY: Governments don't usually pounce on the diplomatic or military missions of other governments.

REDL: If it were outrageous enough.

OBLENSKY: Well, if you can fix it, and it's really scandalous.

REDL: I can.

OBLENSKY: Very well then, fix it, Redl.

(*He hurls his glass into the fireplace where it smashes.*)
Fix it. Now: We've hardly started yet.

FADE

Scene 5

REDL's *apartment in Prague. A beautiful baroque room, dominated by a huge porcelain fireplace and double Central European windows.* VIKTOR *is in bed, naked from the waist up.* REDL *is staring out of the window angrily. Pause.*)

VIKTOR: I think *I'll* get up. . . .

REDL: Why do you make such disgusting scenes with me? If you had the insight to imagine what you look like.

VIKTOR: Oh, don't. (*He flings his blonde head across the pillow.*)

REDL: Oh, stop screaming, you stupid little queen! You don't want to get married, you whore, you urchin! You just want to bleed me to death. You want more. Dear God, if ever there was a ludicrous threat, you don't want the girl or any girl, you couldn't. I've seen her too, remember. *I* could, mark you, and *have*. But not you. When I think . . . How do you imagine you would ever have got a commission in a cavalry regiment, you, who would have bought you three full-blooded horses, and paid your groom and mess bills, *and* taught you to shoot like a gentleman, to behave properly as a Fire leader and be a damned piss-elegant horseman in the field? You couldn't open your mouth and make an acceptable noise of any sort at all. (VIKTOR *weeps softly.*) You're so stupid you thought you could catch me with a shoddy ruse like that. You'll get no bills paid, nor your automobile, that's the bottom of it, you're so avaricious, you'll get nothing. You're so worthless you can't even recognise the shred of petty virtues in others, some of which I have still. Which is why you have nothing but contempt for anyone, like me, who admires you, or loves you, or wants and misses you and has to beg for you at least one day a fortnight. Yesterday, yesterday, I spent two excruciating hours at the most boring party at Möhl's I've ever been to, talking to endless people, couldn't see or hear, hoping you—God knows where you were—that you'd possibly, if I was lucky, might turn up. Just hoping you might look in, so I could light your cigarette, and watch you talking and even touch your hand briefly out of sight.

VIKTOR: I *do* love you.

REDL: In your way, yes. Like a squalling, ravenous, raging child. You want my style, my box at the opera instead of standing with the other officers. You're incapable of initiating anything yourself. If the world depended on the Viktors, on people like you, there would be no first moves made, no inexpedient overtures, no serving, no invention, no spontaneity, no stirring whatsoever in you that doesn't come from elsewhere . . . Dear Mother of God, you're like a woman!

(VIKTOR *howls.* REDL *pulls him out of bed by the leg and he falls heavily to the ground with a thump.*)

You've no memory, no grace, you keep nothing.

(REDL *bends over him.*)

You are thick, thick, a sponge, soaking up. No recall, no fear. You're a few blots . . . All you are is young. There's no soft fat up here in the shoulder and belly and buttocks yet. But it will. Nobody loves an old, squeezed, wrinkled pip of a boy who was gay once. Least of all people like me

or yourself. You'll be a vulgar fake, someone even toothless housewives in the market place can bait. (*Grabs his hair and drags him.*)
You little painted toy, you puppet, you poor duffer, you'll be, with your disease and paunch and silliness and curlers and dyed wispy hair and long legs and varicose veins like bunches of grapes and prostate and thick waist and rolling thighs and big bottom, that's where we all go.
(*Slaps his own.*)
In the bottom, that's where we all go and you can't mistake it. *Everyone'll see it!*
(*He pauses, exhausted. His dressing gown has flown open.* VIKTOR *is sobbing very softly and genuinely.* REDL *stands breathless, then takes the boy's head in his arms. He rocks him. And whispers*):
It's not true. Not true. You *are* beautiful. . . . You always will be. . . . There, baby, there. . . . Baby. . . . It won't last . . . All over, baby. . . .

FADE

Scene 6

Office of GENERAL VON MÖHL, TAUSSIG *is handing papers to the dazed* GENERAL.

TAUSSIG: This is the envelope, sir. As you see, it's addressed
to Nicolai Strach, c/o General Postal Delivery,
Vienna. It lay there for several weeks before it was
opened by the Secret Police, who found it con-
tained five thousand kronen and the names of two
well-known espionage cut-outs, one in Dresden and
another in Paris. The letter was re-sealed. Rumpler
was informed immediately and we waited.

MÖHL: And?

TAUSSIG: Redl took three days' leave and motored in his
automobile to Vienna where he picked up the
letter. On Thursday evening.
(Pause.)

MÖHL: Redl?
(He might almost have burst into tears.)

TAUSSIG: Sir. Then. His account at the Austro-
Hungarian Bank, unpaid bills for stabling, furniture,
tailoring, *objets d'art* and so on. Automobile mainten-
ance, totalling some fifty thousand crowns. Assets:
a little over five, plus valuable personal properties
as yet unvalued. Some securities worth perhaps
eight thousand kronen. His servant Max is owed a
year's wages, but doesn't seem to mind. A trunk
full of photographs, women's clothes, underwear,
etc., love letters to various identified and
unidentified men, a signed oath from Lieutenant

Jerzabek, swearing not to marry during Redl's lifetime and only afterwards by way of certain complicated financial losses in Redl's will. Redl's will . . .

MÖHL: All right. General Von Hötzendorf must be informed at once. No: I must do it. He'll go out of his mind. Redl! How people will enjoy this, they'll enjoy this. The *élite* caught out! Right at the centre of the Empire. You know what they'll say, of course? About the *élite*.

TAUSSIG: Perhaps it can be kept a secret, sir. Do you think? It's still possible.

MÖHL: Yes. We must do it now. Where is Redl?

TAUSSIG: The Hotel Klomser.

MÖHL: We'll see Hötzendorf, get his permission, and then we'll go there, together, you and I. We'll need a legal officer, Kunz I'd say. But he *must* be sworn to outright secrecy. Those damned newspapers. . . .

TAUSSIG: Kunz is the man for that, sir.

MÖHL: Very well. Let's break the news to General Hötzendorf.

FADE

Scene 7

REDL's *bedroom at the Hotel Klomser. Above his bed the black, double-headed eagle of Austria and a portrait of Francis Joseph.* REDL *is seated at a bureau. In front of him stand* MÖHL, TAUSSIG *and* KUNZ. REDL *signs a document, gives it to* KUNZ, *who examines it, then puts it into his briefcase which he straps up briskly.*

KUNZ: That's all, General Möhl. . . .

REDL: You know, General, I know you'll be offended if
   I say this because I know you're a deeply religious
   man, and I . . . well, I've always felt there was a
   nasty, bad smell about the Church. Worse than the
   Jews, certainly. As you know, I'm a Catholic
   myself. Who isn't? Born, I mean.
   (*He takes the champagne bottle out of the bucket and pours
   a glass.*)
   Born. But I think I hate the Spaniards most of all.
   Perhaps that's the flaw . . . of my character . . .
   they *are* Catholics. Those damned Spaniards were
   the worst marriage bargain the Habsburgs ever
   made. Inventing bridal lace to line coffins with.
   They really are the worst. They stink of death, I
   mean. It's in their clothes and their armpits, quite
   stained with it, and the worst is they're so proud
   of it, insufferably Like people with stinking breath
   always puff and blow and bellow an inch away
   from your face. No, the Spaniards are, you must
   admit, a musty lot, the entire nation from top to
   bottom smells of old clothes in the bottom of trunks.
   (MÖHL *motions to* TAUSSIG, *who hands him a revolver.*

122

MÖHL *places it in the bureau in front of* REDL. *Pause.*)

TAUSSIG: Are you acquainted with the Browning pistol, Redl?

REDL: No. I am not.

(TAUSSIG *takes out the Browning Manual and hands it to* REDL.)

Thank you, Taussig. Gentlemen . . .

(*They salute and go out.* REDL *pours another glass of champagne and settles down to read the manual.*)

FADE

Scene 8

A street outside the Klomser Hotel. Early morning. MÖHL,
TAUSSIG *and* KUNZ *wait in the cold.* REDL's *light is visible.*

TAUSSIG: *(looks at watch).* Five hours, General. Should we
go up?

MÖHL: No.

KUNZ: Forgive me, gentlemen. I'm going home. My
wife is waiting for me. My work seems to be done.

MÖHL: Of course.

KUNZ: Good night.

(A shot rings out. They stare. KUNZ *moves off.)*

MÖHL: Well . . .

(They light a cigarette.)

FADE

Scene 9

A Chamber of Deputies. Vienna. Deputies. In the background blow-ups of The Times *for May 30th 1913, headed* 'SUICIDE OF AN AUSTRIAN OFFICER (FROM A CORRESPONDENT) VIENNA. MAY 29.'
(*Facsimiles available from British Museum Newspaper Library.*)

DEPUTY: The autopsy showed the bullet had penetrated the oral cavity, passing obliquely through the brain from left to right. Death must have been practically instantaneous due to haemorrhage. The question is, not who gave this officer the manual, but who allowed him to be given a revolver for this purpose at all?

MINISTER: There will be no concealment of any irregularities.

DEPUTY: Is it not true that this officer was exposed by reason of his official contacts with certain confidential elements in the military-political sphere for a period of some years, with special duties in connection with the frontier protection and the order of armament?

DEPUTY: Was not this same officer in the confidence of von Moltke the Chief of the Imperial German High Command?

DEPUTY: Surely someone must have been around with the wit or perception to have suspected something . . .

DEPUTY: Are we all asleep or what!

(ROAR.)

DEPUTY: *What's become of us?*

(ROARS.)

DEPUTY: Is it not true that he was, in fact, the son of one
Marthe Stein, a Galician Jewess?
(UPROAR.)
Why was this fact not taken note of?
MINISTER: The high treason which General Staff
Colonel Redl was able to practise with impunity
for a period of many years is an occasion of the
gravest possible public disquiet, which is far from
being allayed, if not actually increasing. This is due
not only to the abominable crime committed by
this officer—but more by the way in which the
case has been managed by the authorities of the
Royal and Imperial Army.
DEPUTY: Yes, but what do you *do* about it? What do
you *do*?
MINISTER: We must not alarm the public more than is
necessary. It is true that the crime committed by
Colonel Redl against his country and the uniform
he wore is felt in the most sensitive way by the
whole population. However, the only adequate
protection of the honour of officers lies in rigid
standards, and if individuals act against the
honour of that class, the only helpful thing is the
expulsion from it of those individuals by all the
forms prescribed by law. . . .

FADE

Scene 10

OBLENSKY'S *office. Lights dimmed.* STANITSIN *working the magic lantern.*

OBLENSKY: Next!
   (*A photograph is snapped on to the screen.*)
STANITSIN: Schoepfer. Julius Gerhard. M.D., Ph.D.,
   F.R.C.S., Member Institute Neuro Pathology,
   Vienna. Member Vienna Institute. Hon. Fellow of
   the Royal Society of London. Born Prague March
   25th 1871. Family Jewish. Distinguished patients.
   List follows. Political and Military. In 1897, at the
   age of twenty-five he delivered a brilliant lecture
   on the origins of nervous diseases. . . .

FADE

END OF PLAY

CUTS AND ALTERATIONS
REQUESTED BY THE LORD CHAMBERLAIN

Act I–1   'His spine cracked in between those thighs.
            Snapped. . . . All the way up.'

    I–4   This scene must not be played with the couple
            both in bed.

    I–4   From: Stage direction – She moves over to the
                        wall. . . .
            To: . . . . Presently, he turns away and sits on
                        the bed.

    I–5   Reference to 'clap' and 'crabs'.

    I–7   Reference to 'clap'.

    I–10   Omit the whole of this scene.

    II–1   Omit the whole of this scene.

    III–1 The two men must not be in bed together.

    III–1 From: 'You'll never know that body like I know
                    it. . . .'
            To: '. . . you've not looked at him, you never
                        will.'

    III–1 From: 'So: you'll turn Stefan . . .'
            To: '. . . than any ordinary man.'

    III–2 'You were born with a silver sabre up your what-
            not.'

    III–4 'Tears of Christ!'

    III–5 Omit the whole of this scene.

128